IN PRAISE OF EDWARD DE BONO

"Edward doesn't just think. He is a one-man global industry, whose work is gospel in government, universities, schools, corporates and even prisons all over the world." *Times 2*

"The master of creative thinking." *Independent on Sunday*

"Edward de Bono is a cult figure in developing tricks to sharpen the mind." *The Times*

"Edward de Bono is a toolmaker, his tools have been fashioned for thinking, to make more of the mind." *Peter Gabriel*

"de Bono's work may be the best thing going in the world today." *George Gallup, originator of the Gallup Poll*

"The guru of clear thinking." *Marketing Week*

www.edwarddebono.com

D1114530

CREATIVITY WORKOUT

**62 Exercises to Unlock
Your Most Creative Ideas**

Edward de Bono

Ulysses Press

Published in the United States by
ULYSSES PRESS
P.O. Box 3440
Berkeley, CA 94703
www.ulyssespress.com

First published in Great Britain as *How to Have Creative Ideas* in 2007 by Vermilion, an imprint of Ebury Publishing, a division of the Random House Group

ISBN10: 1-56975-640-6
ISBN13: 978-1-56975-640-9
Library of Congress Catalog Number: 2007905467

Printed in the Canada by Webcom

10 9 8 7 6 5 4 3

Cover design: what!design @ whatweb.com

U.S. editorial and production: Lauren Harrison, Elyce Petker, Emma Silvers, Steven Schwartz

Distributed by Publishers Group West

CONTENTS

Introduction   1

How to Use this Book   9

How to Use Random Words   14

Exercises   17

Tables of Random Words   153

Number Maps   167

Tables of Random Numbers   171

Pre-set Table   174

About the Author   176

INTRODUCTION

Everyone wants to be creative.

Everyone should want to be creative. Creativity makes life more fun, more interesting and more full of achievement.

Research shows that 94 percent of youngsters rate "achievement" as the most important thing in their lives. Creativity is the key skill needed for achievement.

Without creativity there is only repetition and routine. These are highly valuable and provide the bulk of our behavior—but creativity is needed for change, improvement and new directions.

In business, creativity has become essential. This is because everything else has become a commodity available to everyone.

If your only hope of survival is that your organization will continue to be more competent than your competitors, that is a weak position. There is nothing you can do to prevent your competitors also becoming competent.

Information has become a commodity available to everyone. Current technology has become a commodity, with a few exceptions—where a 16-year patent life offers some protection.

Imagine a cooking competition with several chefs at a long table. Each chef has the same ingredients and the same cooking facility. Who wins that competition?

At a lower level the chef with the highest quality wins. But at the higher level all chefs have excellent quality. So who wins? The chef who can turn the same ingredients into superior quality.

In business, competing with India and China on a price basis is impossible. That leaves creating new value as the basis for competition. And that needs a more serious commitment to creativity than is the case at the moment.

CREATIVITY AS TALENT

Too many people believe that creativity is a talent with which some people are born and the rest can only envy. This is a negative attitude that is completely mistaken.

Creativity is a skill that can be learned, developed and applied.

I have been teaching creative thinking for over 30 years to a wide variety of people:

. . . from four-year-olds to 90-year-olds
. . . from Down's syndrome children to Nobel laureates
. . . from illiterate miners in Africa to top executives

Using just one of the techniques of "*lateral thinking*," a group of workshops generated 21,000 ideas for a steel company in one afternoon.

UNINHIBITED

An ordinary man is walking down the road. A group of people seize him and tie him up with a rope. Then a violin is produced. Obviously, the man tied up with the rope cannot play the violin. So what do we say? We claim that if the rope was cut the man would play the violin. This is clearly nonsense. Cutting the rope does not make the man a violinist.

Unfortunately we have the same attitude towards creativity. If you are inhibited it is difficult to be creative. Therefore if we make you uninhibited you will be creative!

This is the basis of "brainstorming" and other popular techniques. There is some merit in these systems but the approach is a very weak one. The formal and deliberate "tools" of lateral thinking are much more powerful.

The brain is designed to be "non-creative." If the brain were creative, life would be impossible. With 11 pieces of clothing to put on in the morning there are 39,916,800 ways of getting dressed. If you tried one way every minute you would need to live to be 76 years old, using your entire waking life trying ways of getting dressed.

Fortunately for us, the brain is designed to form stable patterns for dealing with a stable universe. That is the excellence of the brain and for that we should be very grateful.

So removing inhibition is of value, but only a weak way of developing creativity.

CREATIVITY AS SKILL

Creativity is a skill that everyone can learn, practice and use.

It is as much a skill as skiing, playing tennis, cooking or learning mathematics.

Everyone can learn such skills. In the end not everyone is going to be equally good at these skills. Some people cook better than others. Some people play tennis better than others. But everyone can learn the skill. And everyone can seek to get better through practice.

CREATIVITY IS NOT A MYSTERY

For the first time in history we can now look at creativity as the "logical" behavior of a certain type of information system. The mystery and mystique can be removed from creativity.

1. **We need to look at the human brain as a "self-organizing information system."**
2. **Self-organizing information systems form patterns.**
3. **All pattern-making systems are "asymmetric."**
4. **This is the basis of humor and of creativity. Humor is by far the most significant behavior of the human brain because it indicates the nature of the underlying system. Reason tells us very little because any "sorting system" run backwards is a reasoning system. Humor indicates asymmetric patterns. This means that the route from A to B is not the same as the route from B to A.**

"Lateral thinking" is the creativity concerned with changing ideas, perceptions and concepts. Instead of working harder with the same ideas, perceptions and concepts, we seek to change them. This "idea creativity" is not the same as "artistic creativity," which is why a new term was needed.

All these things are explained in my books on lateral thinking; an understanding of such systems is the logical basis for the practical tools of lateral thinking.

THE WORD "CREATIVE"

In the English language, the word "create" means to bring into being something that was not there before.

So someone can "create a mess." That means bringing into existence a mess that did not exist before. Is that person "creative"?

We hasten to add that what has been brought into existence must have "value." So creativity is bringing into existence something that has value.

There is, of course, the element of "newness" because repetition—no matter how valuable—is not seen as creative.

The word "creative" has largely been taken over by the arts, because in the arts all the work is new and has value. It is true that the value is not always recognized at first. For example, the Impressionist painters were not fully appreciated in their time.

In the English language there does not exist a separate word to distinguish the creativity of new ideas from the creativity of art. So when I claim that "creativity" can indeed be taught, I am asked if Beethoven could be produced in this way. The answer is "no," but "idea creativity" can be taught, learned and developed in a formal way. The purpose of the exercises in this book is to help develop creative habits of mind.

The "creativity" of the art world includes a large element of "aesthetic judgement." The artist judges that something is "right." This is quite different from the ability to produce new ideas. While artists may be excellent in their field, they are not especially good at changing ideas and creating new ideas.

This language problem has two very serious consequences.

The first consequence is that education authorities believe that they are "teaching creativity" by encouraging dancing and music-playing. This is totally wrong. These activities are of value in themselves but they are not teaching creativity.

The second consequence is that people say that if you cannot produce a Beethoven to order, then creativity cannot really be taught. This is also garbage. Idea creativity can be taught.

As a matter of interest, my work is used quite widely in the arts world, particularly in music. Because music does not represent existing sounds, there is a great need for creativity rather than just expression.

HABITS OF MIND

There is no sharp distinction between a mental skill and a mental habit. The two overlap and blend into each other. The purpose of this book is to provide opportunity for practising the mental skill of creativity and developing the habits of mind that make creativity happen.

Suppose you developed the habit of mind of trying to find alternative meanings for well-known acronyms.

So when you looked at NASA, you did not only think of the North American Space Agency, but of other possibilities:

Not Always Same Astronaut
Not Always Same Ascent
Not Always Same Ambition

Or:

New Adventures Splendid Achievements
New Ambitions Serious Attainments

As with a joke, the new explanation is more powerful if it links in with existing knowledge, or even prejudice, about the organization.

POSSIBILITY

Educational establishments totally underestimate the importance of "possibility."

Two thousand years ago, China was far ahead of the West in science and technology. They had rockets and gunpowder. Had China continued at the same rate of progress, then today China would easily have been the dominant power in the world.

What happened? What brought progress to a halt?

The Chinese scholars started to believe you could move from "fact to fact." So they never developed the messy business of possibility (hypothesis, etc.). As a result, progress came to a dead end.

Exactly the same sort of thing is happening in the world today. Because of the excellence of computers, people are starting to believe that all you need to do is to collect data and analyze it. This will give you your decisions, your policies and your strategies. It is an extremely dangerous situation, which will bring progress to a halt. There is a huge need for creativity to interpret data in different ways; to combine data to design value delivery; to know where to look for data; to form hypotheses and speculations, etc., etc.

I have held academic positions at the universities of Oxford, Cambridge, London and Harvard. I have to say that at each of these wonderful institutions the amount of time spent on the fundamental importance of possibility was zero.

Our culture and habits of thinking insist that we always move towards certainty. We need to pay equal attention to possibility.

Peptic ulcer (stomach or duodenal ulcer) is a serious condition that affects many people. Sufferers used to be on antacids for 20 years or more. There were major operations to remove part or all of the stomach. A large number of beds were occupied by patients under treatment or diagnosis of the condition. Hundreds of people were researching this serious condition.

Then a young doctor, Barry J. Marshall, in Perth, Western Australia, suggested that peptic ulcer might be an infection. Everyone laughed, because the hydrochloric acid in the stomach would surely kill any bacteria. No one took the possibility seriously. Many, many years later it turned out that he was right. Instead of antacids for 20 years and losing some or all of your stomach, you simply take antibiotics for one week!

Possibility is very important. And possibility is the key to creativity.

HOW TO USE
THIS BOOK

There is no way you can learn a skill if you do not practice the skill. There is no short cut. There is no other way to develop skill. This holds for the skill of creativity.

There is no magic fountain that you can drink from in order to become creative. The nearest equivalent would be to read this book!

The use of creativity and the practice of creativity are the best ways to develop the mental skills and the mental habits of creative thinking.

If you want to become good at golf, you had better practice hitting the ball. If you want to develop the skill of cooking, you had better get into the kitchen. If you really want to develop the skill of creative thinking, you had better treat this book seriously and work through it diligently and systematically. It is not much use reading the book for knowledge or to find out how the story ends. That's like going to the gym to watch other people exercise. The more you practice, the better you will get—as with golf or cooking.

The book is designed to be simple, practical and usable. The subject of creativity could be made very complicated, but then the book would have no value except to academics. The book is, however, designed for everyone who wants to become more creative and who is willing to enjoy the process.

The book is designed around a series of exercises. You can do the exercises on your own. You can do the exercises with other people. You can use the exercises to practice a little bit of creativity every day.

EXERCISES/GAMES

The purpose of the exercises in this book is to provide training in creative thinking. The attitudes, habits and skills of creative thinking will be developed as you go through the exercises systematically and in a disciplined way.

There are those who believe that any disciplined or systematic approach is the opposite of creativity. This view is complete garbage and shows a lack of understanding of the fundamental nature of creative thinking as the behavior of a self-organizing informational system that makes asymmetric patterns.

At the same time, the exercises are enjoyable and so can be regarded as "games." Generally you would play these games on your own (as with a crossword) and get a sense of achievement when you succeed. It is also possible, occasionally, to play with others and to compare your results.

So, they are enjoyable exercises that could be called either "exercises" or "games." The intention is to train your creative mind.

The book is a playground. If there were a playground with a ball in it, you would certainly kick the ball around. That is the way you should treat this book.

Have fun. But it is serious fun. Creativity is a very serious skill. Unlike many other skills, you can have fun while you develop this serious skill.

From this point onward, it is up to you. What you get out of the book will be directly proportional to the effort you put into using the book.

There are 62 exercises in the book. That means 52 + 10. That suggests that you could, if you wished, practice one exercise one week and the next exercise the following week. The 10 extra exercises are in case you feel extra energetic and want to do more than one exercise that week.

PROBLEMS AND SITUATIONS

Use the given problems and situations even if you find them difficult.

You may also insert problems and situations of your own. Only do this after you have attempted to use the given problems. Otherwise you will tend only to work on easy problems you have chosen.

TIME LIMITS

The exercises may be done without any time limit at all.

You can also set a time limit. To begin with, this could be four to five minutes per exercise.

As you get better, the time limit can be reduced to two to three minutes.

RIGHT ANSWERS

With creativity, there is no one "right answer."

For the exercises there is no one right answer. Any answer that fits the stated requirements of the exercise is equally right. Players will, however, learn to recognize that some answers are indeed better than others—because they are more practical, more unusual, or offer a higher value.

> **NOTE: The fact that there are no right answers does NOT mean that any answer will do. The answer must satisfy the requirements of the exercise.**

If you were asked to suggest "food for breakfast," there is no one right answer. But if you were to suggest "the transmission of a car," that would indeed be a wrong answer.

If you are asked for "alternative modes of transport" and you suggested "a frying pan," that would indeed be a wrong answer.

In the course of the book you will practice both perceptual creativity and constructive creativity.

Perceptual creativity involves looking at things in different ways. It involves extracting concepts. It involves extracting values. It involves opening up connections and associations.

Constructive creativity means putting things together to deliver value. This is "design thinking." While education focuses a great deal on analysis, there is practically no attention at all to design thinking. Yet life and human progress depend on design thinking. Analysis is important, just as the rear left wheel of a car is important—but it is not enough.

Readers of this book will develop creative habits of mind and a fluency in dealing with ideas, concepts, perceptions and values. The emphasis is on the creativity of "what can be" rather than the usual education emphasis on "what is."

ONE A DAY

Many people do some physical exercises every day. Some people go to the gym every day.

I would suggest that you make a habit of doing at least one of the exercises every day.

You should be able to go back to the book again and again to repeat exercises (using different problems, etc.). The book is like a gym for creative thinking habits and skills. And, as with physical exercise, the important thing is to be disciplined about it.

1. Choose an exercise.
2. Set a time limit.
3. Do the exercise.

HOW TO USE RANDOM WORDS

The whole book is based on Random Words. So it is important to understand how to use these.

A Random Word is there for no reason at all—it is random. The words are all nouns because these are easier to use.

The Tables of Random Words are given on pages 155–165.

You can get your Random Word in a number of different ways:

1. **You can throw a single die four times.**
   . . . the first throw indicates which of the six tables you are going to use
   . . . the second throw indicates which column you are going to use
   . . . the third throw indicates which section you are going to use in the column
   . . . the fourth throw indicates which word you are going to use in the section

   You can also throw four dice all at once and then arrange them in a sequence. You can use colored dice with a given sequence of colors.

2. You can use the Number Maps given on pages 167–169. With your eyes closed, stab with a pencil, matchstick or toothpick at the map. Take the number you have hit. If you are on a dividing line or miss a number, simply try again. Do this four times to obtain the four numbers (table number, column number, group number and word number).

3. Use the Tables of Random Numbers given on pages 171–173. Take the numbers in order and tick off the ones you have used. Alternatively, take a sequence from the Tables of Random Numbers and just change one number in the given sequence. You can also create your own Table of Random Numbers in advance so that you can use it whenever you want.

4. Simply invent a sequence of numbers. Each number must be between 1 and 6. Use these numbers as if thrown with a die.

5. In the Pre-set Table (pages 174–175) the sequences of numbers are already given. You can insert your own number (1 to 6) in the gap to give the new sequence.

VERY IMPORTANT: Do not keep trying different Random Words until you get one you like. This destroys the whole point of the exercises. You must seek to use the first word you obtain. If, however, you do not understand the meaning of a Random Word, ignore that word and try again, or else take the next word down.

POWERFUL TOOL

The Random Word process on which the book is built is just one of the powerful tools of lateral thinking which is a process I invented in 1967. The process is now widely used and the phrase has an entry in the *Oxford English Dictionary*.

There are other powerful tools of lateral thinking such as: challenge; concept extraction; concept fan; provocation and movement, etc.

Lateral thinking is serious and systematic creativity. It is not being different for the sake of being different. It is not based on sitting on a river bank and playing Baroque music. It is not a matter of messing around in a brainstorming session. There are formal tools and processes that can be used deliberately and with discipline. These tools are based on the understanding of self-organizing information systems, as described in my book *The Mechanism of Mind* (1969).

For the first time in human history we can treat creativity as a mental skill, not just a matter of talent or inspiration.

PROVOCATION

In a way the Random Word process is an example of provocation.

In normal thinking there needs to be a reason for saying something before it is said. Otherwise the result is nonsense.

With provocation, there may not be a reason for saying something until after it is said.

Develop your creative thinking skills. It's up to you!

EXERCISES

EXERCISE 1

RANDOM INPUT

This is much more than an exercise. This is a serious creative tool. It is one of the basic tools of "lateral thinking." This tool alone was used by a group of workshops to produce 21,000 ideas in an afternoon, for a steel company.

It is the simplest of the creative games or exercises—but by no means the easiest to use.

PROCESS

1. You clearly define your focus. Where and why do you want new creative ideas? It is important to be very clear about the focus. If you do not know what you are shooting at, you are rather unlikely to hit the target!
2. You obtain a Random Word from the tables—using any of the methods indicated on pages 15–16.
3. You use the Random Word to stimulate new ideas for the defined focus.

NOTE: There is a need to be disciplined and focused. It is never a matter of messing around and hoping an idea will somehow emerge.

LOGIC

Logicians tend to get very upset with this method. If the word is random, then any Random Word would help. So any Random Word would help with any focus. This seems to be a definition of "nonsense."

Yet in a "patterning system" the process is indeed logical.

Imagine you live in a smallish town. Whenever you leave home, you always take the main street to get to your destination. One day, on the outskirts of the town, your car breaks down or you have an accident. For some reason you have to walk home. You ask around for directions. You find yourself arriving home by a street you would never have taken on leaving home.

If you start from the periphery, you can open up paths you would never open up from the center. The Random Word drops you at the periphery. As you think your way back to the focus, you open up new ideas.

Along with the other techniques of lateral thinking, the Random Input method was first described by me in 1972 in my book *Lateral Thinking: a Textbook of Creativity*. There have since been many copiers of the idea.

USE OF THE METHOD

1. You should not just look for some sort of connection between the Random Word and the focus. This does not have any stimulating effect at all. The task is not to connect the two, but to use the Random Word for stimulation.

2. You should not rearrange the letters of the Random Word or use the letters as an acronym. Take the word as it is.
3. You should not take a series of steps in order to arrive at a new Random Word. You should not say (for example): "Ship suggests sea; sea suggests navigation; navigation suggests stars—so let's use the word 'stars.'"
4. You will probably need to work in concepts and values rather than simple associations.
5. At every point, look out for possibilities, values and new directions. Once a possibility has emerged, pursue that possibility.
6. Never, never, never say: "I do not like that Random Word, I am going to get another one." You need to force yourself to use the original Random Word. Otherwise you will simply be waiting for an easy connection and you will not stimulate new ideas at all.

RESULTS

Your new idea may do one of several things:

1. Solve a given problem.
2. Offer an improvement or simplification of a process.
3. Provide a new idea.
4. Open up a whole new direction.
5. Define a new concept.
6. Define a new value.

EXAMPLE

The Task is: To provide a new idea for a new restaurant.

The Random Word is: CLOAK.

Immediate thoughts:

. . . a highway robbery theme
. . . a Venetian theme with projected pictures of gondolas
. . . waiters and waitresses to be masked

Further thoughts:

. . . no menu. You tell the head waiter roughly what you feel
    like. He or she then decides your meal for you
. . . you cannot see the food you are eating (it is cloaked).
    Restaurants all in the dark already exist
. . . a vegetarian restaurant, but the food is disguised as
    meat
. . . there are code words you use for ordering the meal

It is clear that two directions have emerged. The first direction
is a "theme" direction associated with "cloak."

The second direction is to do with the concept of "cloaked,"
"masked," "disguised" or "hidden."

TASKS

Here are four tasks for you to tackle. You can always define and
insert a task of your own. This may be a "problem" or just an
area in which you want new ideas.

1. New ideas to make a bank more attractive to its customers.
2. The problem of graffiti being painted on buildings in a town.
3. The problem of cars going too fast along a straight stretch of road.
4. New ideas for a newspaper.

SUGGESTION

It is useful to jot down your ideas. Perhaps you could even keep a log book of your ideas and your progress.

EXERCISE 2

DOUBLE EFFECT

This is a variation of Exercise 1 but it requires much more creative effort.

Two focuses are defined at the same time.

One Random Word is obtained.

The task is to see how the same Random Word can provide ideas for each one of the focuses.

> **NOTE: It may be the same concept that is extracted from the Random Word and then applied to each of the focuses.**
>
> **It may be a different concept that is extracted from the Random Word for each of the different focuses.**

EXAMPLE

Focus 1: "traffic lights."

Focus 2: "burglary."

The Random Word is: VALUE.

Immediate thoughts:

. . . value needs to be seen in advance. So some advanced
way of knowing what the traffic lights are going to do
next

. . . some way of letting burglars know in advance that there
is nothing worth stealing in the house. Perhaps a visible
insurance certificate

Further thoughts:

. . . values depend on circumstances. So traffic light behavior
should depend on the time of day and the state of
traffic

. . . goods are of no value to a burglar if they cannot be
resold. So some invisible spray that could identify
stolen items so the ultimate seller would be held
responsible

EXERCISE 3

ODD MAN OUT

This is a very simple exercise. It is related to those I designed for children in the Think Link series of cards in the early 1970s. (Think Link cards, which show a word or picture, were used randomly to stimulate ideas.)

PROCESS

1. Obtain four Random Words.
2. On some basis show that one of the words is the "odd man out."
3. Define that basis.

> **NOTE:** It is best to avoid the very obvious reasons for one word being the odd man out. These obvious reasons would include: the number of letters; starting or ending with a certain letter, etc. Reasons based on the physical nature of the spelling or the word are best avoided.

EXAMPLE

The four Random Words are: FUR; RANSOM; CHIMPANZEE; WORRY.

Immediate thoughts:

. . . "worry" is the only human emotion among the words
. . . "chimpanzee" is the only creature

Further thoughts:

. . . "ransom" is the only word that implies criminality
. . . "fur," "ransom" and "worry" are all unpleasant (for some people). "Chimpanzee" is not

VARIATIONS

1. The game can be played so that for the same set of Random Words you have to choose a second odd man out.
2. The game can be played so that for the same set of Random Words each of the words could be shown to be an odd man out.

EXERCISE 4

GROUPING

This is another simple exercise that comes from the Think Link series of games published in the early 1970s.

Once again the creative process involves examining the concepts, associations and functions of each of the obtained Random Words.

PROCESS

1. Obtain six Random Words.
2. Divide the six Random Words into two groups of three on some basis.
3. Explain the basis for the grouping.

> NOTE: As before, avoid grouping on an alphabetical basis such as number of letters, beginning letter or ending letter, etc. Seek to deal with the meaning of the words, not the appearance.

EXAMPLE

The six Random Words are: TEARS; NIGHT; PREJUDICE; SPINACH; ANGLE; PAJAMAS.

Immediate thoughts:

. . . "prejudice," "night" and "tears" are dark in nature and the others are not

. . . "angle," "tears" and "prejudice" are all ways of looking at something

Further thoughts:

. . . "prejudice," "spinach" and "tears" can all be complicated. The others are not

VARIATIONS

1. Use the same Random Words but seek to obtain different groupings on differing bases.
2. Use four, or eight, words to start with.
3. Divide the Random Words (six or more) into three groupings on some basis.

EXERCISE 5

PAIRING

Another simple exercise from the Think Link series.

Although it seems very simple, there are times when this exercise will require a lot of creative thought—when you go beyond the obvious.

PROCESS

1. Obtain two lists of four Random Words each. These are List A and List B.
2. On some basis pair a word from List A with a word from List B.
3. Define the basis for the pairing.

   NOTE: As before, avoid simple appearances, number of letters, etc.

EXAMPLE

List A: TOAST; PROPHET; CHIP; TAIL.

List B: RUNWAY; FORMULA; LOLLIPOP; PYRAMID.

Immediate thoughts:

. . . "toast" and "lollipop" are both edible
. . . "prophet" and "pyramid" both occur in ancient cultures
. . . "tail" and "runway" are both to do with airplanes
. . . "chip" and "formula" require mathematics

Further thoughts:

. . . "toast" and "pyramid" can be the same shape
. . . "chip" and "lollipop" are both much liked by children
. . . "tail" and "formula" can both be very long
. . . "prophet" and "runway" suggest departure to the future

VARIATIONS

1. Attempt different pairings (as in the given example).
2. Several words in List A may pair with one word in List B and the other way around. There need not be one word on List B paired with one word on List A.
3. Introduce one further Random Word into List A.

CONNECT

Here the aim is to find a connection. This is rather different from the previous exercises, where the emphasis was more on finding something in common.

What is the connection between the two Random Words?

There may even be an intermediate item that connects the two.

PROCESS

1. **Obtain a list of five Random Words.**
2. **Obtain a further single Random Word.**
3. **Seek to connect the single Random Word with each one of the original five Random Words.**

EXAMPLE

The five Random Words are: CORK; POLITICIAN; MENU;
HAM; POWER.

The single Random Word is: DOCTRINE.

Immediate thoughts:

. . . a doctrine bottles things up and so does a cork
. . . politicians always have their own doctrines
. . . a doctrine has a menu of beliefs and values
. . . some doctrines forbid the eating of ham
. . . doctrines can be used as the basis for power

Further thoughts:

. . . some doctrines forbid alcohol ("cork")
. . . politicians try to make use of religious doctrines
. . . doctrines can shape a menu in a restaurant
. . . doctrines, like ham, can be sliced finely
. . . doctrines make use of the power of belief

VARIATIONS

1. Keep the same five Random Words but obtain a new
   single Random Word and seek to connect as before.
2. For the original set of Random Words seek alternative
   bases for the connections.

EXERCISE 7

COMBINING

The aim here is to combine two different things together to deliver a new value.

The effectiveness of the combination is assessed by whether it can offer value as a business and make profits. That is the measure of effectiveness. An idea that seems interesting but would not form the basis of a business does not qualify in this exercise.

PROCESS

1. **Obtain two Random Words.**
2. **Seek to combine the two words to create a new business. Seek to combine the words as directly as possible rather than just take some aspect from the words.**
3. **Show how the new business would work and why it might be expected to make a profit.**

> **NOTE: The emphasis is on the direct combination of the two items rather than just taking an idea from one of them and applying it to the other (as in some previous exercises).**

EXAMPLE

The Random Words are: DOCK and CABIN.

Immediate thoughts:

. . . special parks where traveling cabins (motor homes) can dock very easily and comfortably

Further thoughts:

. . . creation of special docks for the home ("cabin"). These would be places where you could put various things like cameras, computers, briefcases, etc. Sale of these specially designed "docks"

VARIATIONS

1. Instead of forming a profit-making business by combining the words, you can set up something that provides benefit to people or the environment, even if this does not make profits as a business.
2. Obtain a third word and see if this could be added to the existing combination—or might change the combination.

IMPROVEMENT

Improvement may be in the direction of simplification, greater convenience, reduced costs, etc. Improvement may also mean doing things in a faster way. There are many directions for improvement.

Sometimes improvement means solving problems, large or small, that might exist. But improvement can also take place where there are no obvious problems.

PROCESS

1. **Obtain one Random Word. This is the base word.**
2. **Obtain a second Random Word.**
3. **Seek to show how the second Random Word can be used to improve the process, function or nature of the first Random Word.**
4. **Show how the improvement would work and why it might be feasible.**

NOTE: Seek to use the first Random Word you obtain even if this seems difficult. If it is impossible, obtain another Random Word. But do not just wait for an easy improvement.

EXAMPLE

The first Random Word is: MICROWAVE.

The second Random Word is: SHOE HORN.

Immediate thoughts:

. . . a plastic object shaped something like a shoe horn to get hot dishes out of the microwave oven

Further thoughts:

. . . some way of putting damp shoes in the microwave to dry them out

VARIATIONS

1. Reverse the order. Use the first word to improve the function of the second word.
2. Try a new second Random Word and see if you get very different ideas.

EXERCISE 9

VALUE

Values are central to all behavior. There are many different sorts of values. Values differ with circumstance and from person to person.

This exercise is concerned with picking out and assessing value. Values are often subjective, so your assessment is as valid as anyone else's. There may be a special value for you alone. This is a valid value. That is why creative thinking is important even in this apparent judgement situation.

PROCESS

1. **Obtain five Random Words.**
2. **Define the value base you are using. Some possible value bases are given here. You can add to them as you wish:**

    Most expensive   Most attractive
    Most useful   Most durable
    Most dangerous   Cheapest

3. **Choose one of the Random Words as showing the highest value on your chosen basis.**
4. **Explain your choice.**

NOTE: Values do depend on circumstance. It is possible that in a very special circumstance (for example, someone drowning), one item may have particular value. For this exercise exclude special circumstances and think only of normal circumstances.

EXAMPLE

The five Random Words are: CAP; GRADUATE; CRITIC; CONCRETE; ALGAE.

Immediate thoughts:

. . . the most expensive: graduate
. . . the most useful: concrete
. . . the most dangerous: critic
. . . the cheapest: algae
. . . the most durable: concrete

Further thoughts:

. . . the most personally useful: cap
. . . the most attractive: cap
. . . the one with the most potential: algae

VARIATIONS

1. Choose some value basis and then give a score for each Random Word from one to five.
2. Choose some basis and then rank all the Random Words in order on that basis: first, second, third, etc.

EXERCISE 10

MULTIPLE CONNECTIONS

The obvious answer or idea usually blocks any further ideas. The emphasis in this exercise is on going beyond the obvious.

There may be an obvious connection, but you are invited to go beyond this and to generate as many connections as you possibly can.

This is another exercise from the Think Link series.

PROCESS

1. Obtain two Random Words.
2. See how many ways you can make a connection between the two Random Words.
3. Define clearly the basis for each connection.

NOTE: As usual, avoid simple similarities based on letters, spelling, etc.

EXAMPLE

The first Random Word is: DESK.

The second Random Word is: SHORTS.

Immediate thoughts:

. . . both are functional and aid a type of activity, such as
   business or sports
. . . both should be designed for freedom of activity
. . . desks have "knee holes" and shorts expose the knees

Further thoughts:

. . . both are "expectations." You are supposed to work at a
   desk. You are expected to wear shorts for certain
   activities
. . . traditionally they were both male-associated items. That
   is no longer the case

VARIATIONS

1. Rate each of your connections as "weak" or as "strong."
2. Find special circumstances where new connections
   might apply.

EXERCISE 11

BRIDGE

This is another "connections" exercise. How do you move from one item to another? You can also do this on the basis of something in common, some shared concept or similarity. The exercise is similar to the Concept Snap game in the Think Link series.

The task is to arrange a "bridge" between two chosen ends.

PROCESS

1. **Obtain five Random Words.**
2. **From these five Random Words select two words. These two words are going to form the two ends of the bridge.**
3. **Now arrange the remaining three words to form the bridge. Each word must connect to the word on each side of it, so that you move smoothly along the bridge from one end to the other.**
4. **For each link in the bridge describe clearly the basis for the linkage. Why does this word lead on to the next?**

    NOTE: You are choosing the end words for the bridge and also the order of the linking words. You may need to experiment to get as sound a bridge as you can.

EXAMPLE

The five Random Words are: PANTS; PASSWORD; COMMITTEE; ASPIRIN; COFFIN.

Immediate thoughts:

. . . choice of bridge ends: "aspirin" and "coffin"
. . . "aspirin" to "committee": involving headaches
. . . "committee" to "pants": usually male-dominated
. . . "pants" to "password": recognition among males
. . . "password" to "coffin": death gives everyone the
      password to the next life

Further thoughts:

. . . bridge ends: "committee" and "aspirin"
. . . "committee" to "coffin": lots of dead-weights in a
      committee
. . . "coffin" to "pants": the need to cover up
. . . "pants" to "password": special windows for use
. . . "password" to "aspirin": to unlock inflammatory
      responses

VARIATIONS

1. Use the same set of Random Words but try different ends to the bridge.
2. Choose end words from the original set and then obtain three new Random Words to form the bridge between the end words.
3. Try with six or seven Random Words.

EXERCISE 12

STRING

This exercise is similar in many ways to the Bridge exercise but it is harder because the type of connection is fixed in advance.

The link from one Random Word to the next has to be of the type defined before the exercise is started.

Possible types of link or connection:

Concepts
Functions
Values
Associations
Utility

PROCESS

1.   Define the type of link that is going to be used.
2.   Obtain five Random Words.
3.   Arrange the words in a "string" so that each word leads on from the first word to the next and on to the last word.

EXAMPLE

Chosen link type: Concepts.

The five Random Words are: NET; CUP; SANDALS; HAM; ALUMINIUM.

Immediate thoughts:

... start with "aluminium" and with the concept of "structural support" move on to "sandals"
... from "sandals" move on with the concept of "human convenience" to "cup"
... from "cup" take the functional concept of "container" and move on to "net"
... "net" as in fishing net is designed to help human eating. With this concept we move on to "ham"

Further thoughts:

... start with "ham" and move with the concept of "human design" to "sandals"
... from "sandals" we take the concept of "open design" and move to "net"
... from "net" we take the concept of a "tension structure" and move to "aluminium"
... from "aluminium" we take the concept of "light and strong" and move to "cup"

VARIATIONS

1. Try the same set of words with different types of link.
2. Alternate the link types. Lay out a schedule of link types and then follow this schedule.

EXERCISE 13

STORY LINE

This is another exercise that comes from the Think Link series. It is rather different from the preceding exercises and requires a different sort of creativity. This is "constructive creativity," as distinct from "perceptual creativity."

PROCESS

1. **Obtain four Random Words.**
2. **Create a story using the Random Words in any order you wish to fit the story you want to tell.**

    NOTE: The story should have more interest than just saying: "He went shopping and he bought this and this and this . . ." Or "He was traveling in a bus and saw this and this and this . . ."

EXAMPLE

The four Random Words are: PATROL; WASP; LASSO; DRUG.

Immediate thoughts:

... there was a patrol out to catch people believed to be
smuggling drugs across the border. They were chasing
a man and about to lasso him when a wasp stung the
hand of the person with the lasso. As a result he
lassoed a member of the patrol and the smuggler got
away

Further thoughts:

... the police chief said: "You do not set out to catch a
wasp with a lasso. Trying to catch drug-dealers with a
patrol is just as useless. You need to infiltrate their
network."

VARIATIONS

1. Use the Random Words in the order in which they are
   obtained. You must tell the story with this fixed
   sequence. You cannot choose your own sequence.
2. Use five, six or even seven Random Words.
3. Obtain five Random Words and then choose one to
   throw out and not use. You end up using four Random
   Words for the story and have thrown out the one
   which may not fit.

EXERCISE 14

FORCED STORY

In the previous exercise you could see all the Random Words before you started the story so you could adjust your story. In this exercise you only see the Random Words as they are obtained and must start your story without knowing what comes next.

PROCESS

1. Obtain Random Words one at a time.
2. Start the story when the first two Random Words have been obtained.
3. Obtain the third Random Word and continue the story.
4. Do the same for the fourth and fifth Random Words.

> **NOTE: The storyline must have some substance and not just be a string of "and" followed by "and," etc.**

EXAMPLE

The first two Random Words are: HORSESHOE and FUNERAL.

Immediate thoughts:

. . . there was a funeral and the horse was pulling the hearse with the coffin in it. A horseshoe came off the horse, which stumbled

Next Random Word: SALAD.

. . . the horseshoe flew into the salad of a man eating at a street-side café

Next Random Word: LENTIL.

. . . his companion said to him, "I am glad it did not land in my lentil soup or we would all have been splashed"

Next Random Word: RASH.

. . . he said to her: "Who knows, the lentil soup might have cured that rash you get on your arms. Scientific discoveries are often made that way"

No further thoughts, because the sequence is now known.

VARIATIONS

1.   Obtain six Random Words, two at a time. Choose the order in which you are going to use each of the two words.
2.   After obtaining the first two Random Words, obtain two Random Words for each of the next three stages. Choose to use only one of the two each time and discard the other.

EXERCISE 15

PROBLEM SOLVING

Too many people believe that creative thinking is only for problem-solving. This is a mistake, because creative thinking can produce powerful changes in things that were never problems at all.

Nevertheless, one of the tasks of creative thinking is indeed problem-solving.

The exercise given here is another one from the Think Link series.

PROCESS

1. Define the problem that is going to be solved. This may be a general problem or a specific problem. Some problems are given below. You are invited to use your own problems—but only after you have had some practice on the problems given here:
   . . . thefts from cars in parking lots
   . . . a boy has fallen into the river
   . . . thefts in a supermarket
   . . . traffic congestion in cities
   . . . youngsters drinking too much alcohol

2. Obtain four Random Words.
3. Show how the item indicated in one of the four
   Random Words could help to solve the problem.

NOTE: In this exercise you must seek to use the item
indicated by the Random Word. You must use the item
directly and not use ideas stimulated by the item.

EXAMPLE

Problem: There is difficulty in attracting tourists to a seaside
town.

The four Random Words are: TRACTOR; FABLE; SANITY;
FRANCE

Immediate thoughts:

. . . advertise widely in FRANCE (unless the town happens to
     be in FRANCE)

Further thoughts:

. . . create a fable for the town or area and write this up in
     books, children's books, movies, etc.

VARIATIONS

1. Use just two Random Words to force greater creativity.
2. Show how more than one of the Random Words could
   help solve the problem (with the four Random Words
   of the standard exercise).

EXERCISE 16

IDEAS FOR PROBLEM-SOLVING

This exercise is similar to the preceding exercise, but there is a key difference. In Exercise 15 you were required to use the object indicated by the Random Word to solve the problem.

In this exercise you obtain an idea from the Random Word and then show how this idea can help solve the problem. This use is very similar to that shown in Exercise 1.

PROCESS

1. Define the problem. You can use one of the problems given for Exercise 15. You can also insert a problem of your own.
2. Obtain a single Random Word.
3. See how this Random Word can trigger ideas that might help solve the defined problem.

NOTE: Ideas, concepts or broad concepts can be taken from the Random Word and applied to the problem situation.

EXAMPLE

Defined problem: A seaside town wants to attract more tourists. What can be done?

The Random Word is: JOY.

Immediate thoughts:

. . . organize a "happiness festival" once every year. Give free or subsidized accommodation to people who can prove that they are really happy. Give medals or awards to people who are happy

Further thoughts:

. . . set up a school for training clowns. Employ clowns in restaurants, hotels, etc. Have an annual meeting of clowns

VARIATIONS

1. Obtain two Random Words. Choose to use one of them and discard the other.
2. Obtain two Random Words. Use both of them.

EXERCISE 17

LISTS

The emphasis here is on seeing similarities. What do apparently different things have in common?

PROCESS

1. Obtain three Random Words. Each of these words will now form the heading of a list.
2. Obtain further Random Words one at a time. Each word obtained must be placed in one of the three lists already set up.
3. When a word is placed in a list, the reason for that placement must be declared. What does this word have in common with the list heading?
4. If a new Random Word cannot be placed in a list, the word is put aside.
5. The exercise ends when three Random Words have been put aside.

NOTE: There can be any basis at all for relating a Random Word to the list-heading word.

EXAMPLE

The three Random Words are: MUSTARD (List A); COMPUTER (List B); FALL (List C).

First further Random Word: REFUGEE.

... **"refugee" goes into List C because it is the result of a disaster or a problem and so is related to "fall"**

Second further Random Word: DIVORCE.

... **"divorce" also goes into List C because it is a fall from the happiness of marriage**

Third further Random Word: DOOR HANDLE.

... **"door handle" goes into List B because it is a means to open things up—as is a computer**

Fourth further Random Word: BRA.

... **"bra" goes into List A because mustard is used to make food more attractive and a bra is also used to make shapes more attractive**

Fifth further Random Word: JURY.

... **"jury" goes into List C because a jury is used to try someone who has fallen out of grace with society**

Sixth further Random Word: COAL.

... **"coal" goes into List A because coal has to do with heat and mustard has to do with a hot taste**

Seventh further Random Word: FLEA.

. . . this word could be discarded, or it could go into List A, because a flea is an irritant and mustard gas is also an irritant

The process could continue.

VARIATIONS

1. Have more than three headings.
2. Put a word under more than one heading. You must show the reasons behind this.
3. Have a discard list. The exercise continues until the discard list has more entries than the longest list.

EXERCISE 18

PROGRESSION

With this exercise we are back to "constructive creativity."

The exercise is also about "growing" an organization.

PROCESS

1. Obtain two Random Words. Combine these to form a profit-making business or any other type of organization with a defined purpose.
2. Obtain a further Random Word. This new word is used to grow or add to the existing organization.
3. Obtain two further Random Words, one at a time. In each case, show in what way that word could grow the existing organization.

NOTE: Both the actual use of the item in the Random Word and concepts obtained from the Random Word are acceptable.

EXAMPLE

The first two Random Words are: SPADE; HOBBY.

Immediate thoughts:

. . . many people are involved in DIY both out of necessity and as a hobby. Create a business to employ such people and offer a service to home-owners both inside the house and also in the garden ("spade")

New Random Word: LOOM.

. . . "loom" suggests weaving and cloth, so we can add a service to make curtains, table linen, etc.

New Random Word: HORN.

. . . "horn" suggests a noise as in a car horn. So add to the service ways of insulating houses against the noise of traffic and other noises

New Random Word: AID.

. . . "aid" suggests that the new service would not only do things but would also help and teach people how to do things for themselves

VARIATIONS

1. Discard a Random Word and choose another one.
2. Obtain two Random Words each time but only use one. So you choose the word which is most helpful.

EXERCISE 19

CLUES

This exercise involves "constructive creativity" in the service of fiction.

A murder has been committed and some clues are given. What hypothesis can you construct from the clues?

PROCESS

1. Obtain two Random Words.
2. Use the two Random Words to create the scene, setting or story for a murder. But you must not indicate how the murder took place or who did it.
3. Obtain three further Random Words. These are the clues.
4. Use the clues to construct a reasonable hypothesis of how the murder took place and even who might have done it.

NOTE: You may need to range quite widely around the Random Words that are obtained in order to construct a good story.

EXAMPLE

The first two Random Words are: TIGER; STAIN.

. . . a man was found dead just outside the tiger cage in a
zoo. There was a strange green stain on the front of his
shirt

The Clues are: RHINOCEROS; CORN; CHICKEN.

Thoughts:

. . . He was on his way to give corn to the chickens when he
was charged by a rhinoceros, which had escaped. The
green stain came from his pen, which had been
crushed in his pocket

EXERCISE 20

SUPPORT
FOR AN IDEA

In this exercise the creative effort is directed at seeing how the random input may affect an idea—either positively or negatively.

PROCESS

1. Some idea, suggestion or modification is made. This needs to be clearly defined. Here is a list of possible suggestions. You may also insert your own.
    . . . tax road use directly, so much per mile
    . . . formal education to end at age 14
    . . . abolish universities
    . . . two ministers for each government department: a minister of continuity and a minister of change
    . . . women to propose marriage to men
2. Obtain Random Words, one at a time.
3. For each Random Word obtained, show how this will affect the idea or suggestion. The effect may be positive or negative. The effect may be direct or indirect.

    NOTE: It is not your intention to attack the idea nor to force it through. An objective look at the idea is what is needed.

EXAMPLE

The suggested idea is: "To raise the age at which people receive pensions." Most governments are finding it hard to deliver pensions, since the ratio of young people to old people is changing.

First Random Word: VALLEY.

. . . a valley suggests a dip in the line across a chart. The idea would be to raise the pension age but to make even better provision for those in a "dip" (sick or incapacitated)

Second Random Word: GARDEN.

. . . there may be types of work which old people might enjoy doing—like gardening. There would be a special way of employing old people instead of giving them pensions

Third Random Word: PEARL.

. . . a pearl is unusual and special. There are always special people who are talented and motivated. But not everyone is so special. You need to see how raising the pension age is going to affect most people—not only the special ones

Fourth Random Word: LASSO.

. . . a lasso is always directed at a single animal. So perhaps special pension arrangements could be tailored for individuals. This could be done through choice or depending on circumstances. There need not be a blanket rule for all

VARIATIONS

1. Use a Random Word at the beginning to suggest the theme.
2. Obtain two Random Words each time. Select one of them and discard the other.
3. Decide in advance of each Random Word whether it is going to be used to support the idea or to weaken the idea.

EXERCISE 21

WRITING A NOVEL

This is another exercise involving "constructive creativity." This time it is in the service of fiction.

Note that the use of Random Words in this exercise is very structured and you are expected to follow the given structure.

The purpose of the exercise is to set up the framework of a novel. This means the general framework and not the details.

PROCESS

1. Obtain four Random Words, one at a time. You must use each Random Word as you get it and not wait until all the words are available.
2. The first Random Word indicates the general setting or scene of the novel.
3. The second Random Word suggests the various characters in the novel.
4. The third Random Word suggests the storyline of the novel.
5. The fourth Random Word gives the outcome or ending of the novel.

NOTE: Each Random Word must be used as soon as it is obtained, one by one.

EXAMPLE

First Random Word (setting): SERENADE.

> . . . this suggests a romantic situation. A young man on vacation in Spain falls in love with a beautiful girl in the village

Second Random Word (characters): RIB.

> . . . the girl is the daughter of the local butcher. There is a large family with aunts, uncles, etc. (many ribs)

Third Random Word (storyline): SEAT.

> . . . the young man has always seen the girl sitting down, in a restaurant or café. One day she stands up and is a head taller than him

Fourth Random Word (outcome): VASE.

> . . . he tells her that it is not the vase that matters but what you put in the vase. So it is not her size that matters but her heart and spirit. They marry and live happily ever after

VARIATIONS

1. Obtain all four Random Words at once. Then sort out which word is going to be used for which phase (setting, characters, etc.).

2. At each step of the exercise, instead of obtaining one Random Word, obtain two words and then choose which one you are going to use.
3. For the final outcome, obtain two Random Words. Then devise two outcomes for the novel—one for each of the two Random Words.

EXERCISE 22

CENTRAL

This exercise goes back to "perceptual creativity." You have to look at things in different ways.

You need to be able to perceive a wide range of relationships, similarities, etc.

PROCESS

1. Obtain five Random Words. View them all together.
2. Select from these five words the one you choose to be the most "central."
3. Relate the four other Random Words to the one you have chosen to be central.
4. In each case explain the nature of the relationship.

EXAMPLE

The five Random Words are: KISS; KENNEL; BEANS; REVENGE; WAR.

Immediate thoughts:

. . . "kennel" is chosen as the central word
. . . beans come in cans. The cans are a sort of container or
       kennel for the beans
. . . with war, people and nations get trapped or contained
       within the history of their emotions
. . . a kiss is an invitation to someone to come share your
       kennel (further down the road)
. . . with revenge, a person is contained within a perception
       of history and their emotions. It may be difficult to get
       out

Further thoughts:

. . . "beans" is the central word
. . . war is often about food, oil and the necessities of life.
       "Beans" symbolizes food, etc.
. . . "kennel" is the comfort part of a dog's life, just as beans
       are a comforting food
. . . a kiss is warm, comforting and something you look
       forward to—just like beans
. . . revenge is yours and you wake up with it every morning
       just like you may have beans for breakfast every
       morning

VARIATIONS

1. Seek to make each of the Random Words central in
   turn and then relate the others to this word.
2. Obtain six Random Words and discard one of them
   before proceeding.

DIFFERENT

This is another exercise where you are asked to go beyond the obvious. This, of course, is a key element of creative motivation. There needs to be the effort to go beyond the obvious.

PROCESS

1. Obtain five Random Words and put them down in a list.
2. For each of the Random Words, put down the most immediate response, whether this is an association, a concept, etc.
3. Now return to the list and for each Random Word put down a response which is clearly different from the first one.

NOTE: In all cases the responses must be logical and reasonable and not just arbitrary.

EXAMPLE

Random Word	First response	Second response
SAILOR	ship	girls in ports
FAINT	collapse	feeble sound
FEAST	celebration	gluttony
HARP	angels	to nag
FIGHT	aggression	lively spirit

VARIATIONS

1. Seek to get three or even four different responses from the same Random Word.
2. Avoid conventional double meanings of the same word. (Conventional double meanings are where a word has two possible meanings, such as "maid," which may mean a servant or a young lady.)
3. Mark your own variations as "different" and "very different."

EXERCISE 24

USEFUL

This exercise involves the use of creativity in perception and value. In the end there has to be a real value which affects you directly as a person. That is the best test of value.

PROCESS

1. Obtain six Random Words.
2. Choose which three you would like because they might help you directly in your life.
3. Explain the reasons behind your choices.

> NOTE: You are not allowed to sell any item to raise money. Nor are you allowed to barter or exchange an item for another. You must use the item directly or not at all.

EXAMPLE

The six Random Words are: MICROPHONE; LOLLIPOP;
STREAM; FISH; WALTZ; FROCK.

Thoughts:

... choice of MICROPHONE: I give a lot of lectures and a
   really good microphone would be most useful
... choice of LOLLIPOP: there is always a need for things
   that are simple and enjoyable, so a supply of lollipops
   would be nice
... choice of WALTZ: this is my favorite dance. And there
   would have to be someone I was waltzing with!

VARIATIONS

1. Arrange all six Random Words in the order of
   usefulness to yourself—the most useful at the top.
2. Obtain eight Random Words and select three.

EXERCISE 25

OPPOSITES

There are many sorts of opposites: positive/negative, up/down, right/left, socialist/capitalist, etc., etc.

In this exercise you choose your type of opposite but you need to explain it clearly.

PROCESS

1. Obtain four Random Words.
2. Out of these four, pick two Random Words that you believe to be opposite in some respect.
3. Explain why you consider these words as being opposite to each other: what is the basis?

NOTE: Opposite means in the opposite direction. Just being different is not enough.

EXAMPLE

The four Random Words are: IRON; ANCHOR; ALTAR; NURSERY.

Immediate thoughts:

. . . "nursery" and "altar." The nursery looks after children, who are innocent. The altar or church looks after people who may have sinned and are seeking redemption

Further thoughts:

. . . "iron" and "anchor." Iron can be fashioned into many shapes. It can be altered and changed. An anchor must be secure and never change its hold on the sea bed

VARIATIONS

1. Obtain a single Random Word. Then obtain three more Random Words and see which of these is the most opposite to the first word obtained.
2. See if there is any way in which the four Random Words can be shown each to be the opposite of the others.

LINK BACK

This is rather a difficult exercise. The task is very demanding. A lot of creativity is needed. This is "perceptual creativity."

The term "link back" means "connect" or "have relevance."

PROCESS

1. Lay out five different types of business or five different situations.
2. Obtain a single Random Word.
3. Show how this word links back or connects to each of the businesses or situations that have been laid out.

> **NOTE:** The "link back" should be significant. For example, the word is "light switch." It would not be enough to say that all businesses have buildings and all buildings have light switches in them.

EXAMPLE

The Five Types of Business are: life insurance; motor car sales; travel agent; restaurant; private school.

The Random Word is: PASSPORT.

Thoughts:

. . . a form of passport that a person carries that lists all his insurance policies, etc., especially relating to accidents and disasters

. . . a formal record of the performance and servicing of a motor car—a sort of passport for the car that indicates when servicing is needed, etc.

. . . a second passport held by the travel agent, who can then obtain visas as needed even when the person is traveling

. . . a record that a restaurant keeps for regular customers listing the dishes and wines they have had and enjoyed

. . . "passport" suggests overseas. So the school should make an effort to attract students from all over the world

VARIATIONS

1. Try a second Random Word with the same set of businesses or situations.
2. Obtain two Random Words and then see which one of the two fits for each business or situation.
3. Use Random Words to suggest the five businesses or situations in the first place.

EXERCISE 27

NEEDS

Needs are a sort of value, but they are values that are "needed." Other values may be nice or a luxury, but needs are needed.

This is another exercise in perceptual creativity. How can you look at things in different ways?

PROCESS

1. Start off with a defined list of needs. Create your own or use the one given here in the example.
2. Obtain four Random Words.
3. Examine the four Random Words to see which of them could apply to one or more of the defined needs.
4. Explain how the Random Word would help satisfy that need.

    NOTE: The explanation of how the need might be met needs to be clear and logical.

EXAMPLE

Defined needs: protection; food; shelter; money; friends.

The four Random Words are: WRENCH; ANKLE; SURGEON; BOOK.

Thoughts:

. . . "wrench" or "surgeon" might suggest a type of training or profession which would provide money

. . . "wrench" might suggest a DIY ability to construct your own shelter

. . . "book" might contain recipes for cooking and so make the food more interesting

. . . "book" might also be something you could discuss with friends, or you could make friends through a book club

. . . "wrench" might provide a weapon for protection

. . . "ankle" might suggest a sport where you could make friends

VARIATIONS

1. Pick just one need. Obtain Random Words one by one and seek to show how each might help with that need.
2. Lay out the list of needs. Obtain one Random Word and seek to show how that word could help, directly or indirectly, to supply each of the needs.
3. Select one need. Obtain five Random Words. Rank them in order according to how well they help with that need.

EXERCISE 28

ASSOCIATIONS

In this exercise, the emphasis is directly on associations—not on concepts, functions or values.

The association steps taken must be strong. The steps must be short. The emphasis is not on possibility but on logical associations.

PROCESS

1. Obtain two Random Words.
2. The task is to move from one of the Random Words to the other one using association steps.
3. The steps must be clearly explained.

> NOTE: Concepts are not permitted as steps. Values are not permitted as steps.

EXAMPLE

The two Random Words are: VINEGAR and BANDAGE.

Immediate thoughts:

. . . vinegar is made from wine. Wine contains alcohol. Many
car accidents are caused by alcohol. Victims may need
to be bandaged in some way

Further thoughts:

. . . vinegar goes into salad dressings. Salads are eaten by
vegetarians, who believe that animals should not be
killed for food. Killing involves injury. Bandages are
used for injuries

VARIATIONS

1. Obtain one Random Word and then two more Random
    Words. Using only associations, move from the first
    word to each of the other two.
2. Obtain one Random Word and then two others. Show
    how you can move from each of the two to the original
    one using only associations.

EXERCISE 29

ENJOY

This is another exercise in constructive creativity. There is a definite end value.

The end value is enjoyment or entertainment.

The enjoyment may be formal, as in an organized business, or informal, as in something you would enjoy doing.

PROCESS

1. Obtain five Random Words.
2. Select four of the words and discard the fifth.
3. Show how the four words can be put together to provide enjoyment of some sort—formal or informal.

> **NOTE: There should be an integration of the four words, not just a listing: "I did this and then this and then this," etc.**

EXAMPLE

The five Random Words are: VINE; CARD; JAY; PRANK; CRUMBS.

Thoughts:

. . . discard "prank"
. . . "jay" suggests a bird park
. . . there could be lush vegetation and vines of all sorts
. . . visitors would be given a set of colored cards each of which showed one of the types of birds in the sanctuary. You should try and see them all
. . . the crumbs can be used to feed the birds in the park

VARIATIONS

1. Using the four Random Words (selected from the five obtained), design a profitable type of business relating to vacations or entertainment.
2. Obtain six Random Words. Use three of them to design an entertainment business and the other three to design some form of entertainment which is not a business.
3. Obtain three Random Words and design an entertainment business. Obtain another group of three more Random Words. Show how the new words can improve or extend the original business.

EXERCISE 30

CONTAIN

The emphasis is on containing or absorbing in some way. You may need to be creative to show how this can be done. You are allowed some creative licence in this exercise, which would otherwise be too difficult.

PROCESS

1. Obtain four Random Words.
2. Show how one of these words could contain or absorb the other three.

   NOTE: You are allowed to be imaginative.

EXAMPLE

The four Random Words are: MEADOW; FIGURE;
ENVIRONMENT; SENATOR.

Immediate thoughts:

... the environment includes the meadow, which includes
the figure of the senator walking his dog

Further thoughts:

... the senator in a speech to Congress is talking about the
environment and gives the example of the desecration
of a meadow near his home by shady figures

VARIATIONS

1. Obtain one Random Word. Then obtain others one by
   one until you have three that could be contained or
   absorbed by the first one.
2. Obtain four Random Words. Then obtain further
   Random Words, one by one, until you get one that
   could contain or absorb the original four.

TASK-ACHIEVING

There is a defined task to be carried out. How do you carry it out? This is different from problem-solving. In problem-solving we want to be rid of the problem. With task-achieving we want to achieve something that we believe will deliver value.

PROCESS

1. Define the task to be achieved. You may use one of the tasks given here or choose one of your own:
    . . . making a movie
    . . . designing a theme park
    . . . creating a new type of hat
    . . . setting up riverside entertainment
    . . . picking a team of creative people
    . . . setting up a restaurant.
2. Obtain a single Random Word.
3. How can this Random Word be used to help achieve the defined task? What new directions are opened up?

NOTE: This should be different from problem-solving and the defined tasks should not be problems as such. You may come up with general directions for approaching the task. You may come up with specific concepts. You may even come up with practical detailed ideas. All are valid.

EXAMPLE

The Task is: Setting up a restaurant.

The Random Word is: CLIMBING.

Thoughts:

. . . the restaurant might have a mountaineering theme. You might even have to climb to reach your table

. . . "climbing" in terms of setting up the restaurant might mean starting with a simple café and then building upwards, getting experience on the way before opening the full-scale restaurant

. . . climbers on a mountain are roped together and help each other. So it might be a matter of finding partners and tying everyone into the project with agreements and contracts

. . . "climbing" suggests there is a mountain to be climbed. This may mean defining very clearly what the restaurant will be like—and how it might differ from other restaurants. The vision should be clear to everyone

VARIATIONS

1. Obtain two Random Words and show how each one opens up a different route or direction.
2. Obtain two Random Words but discard one of them and use the other.
3. Seek to show how the same Random Word can suggest alternative approaches to achieving the task.

EXERCISE 32

NEW SPORT

This is a design exercise with a defined task. The task is one that is full of needed values. A sport has to be safe, fun to play, good to watch, easy to start, have high skill at later levels, etc., etc.

This is very different from just creating something new and different and believing that novelty is a sufficient value.

Most sports (football, hockey, cricket, baseball, basketball, etc.) have been around a long time. Perhaps it is time for a new sport!

PROCESS

1. Define the objective as given above. You may also add that it should be a field sport or a two-person sport, etc., or you can leave this open.
2. Obtain three Random Words.
3. Use one or all the Random Words to design the new sport.
4. Lay out the benefits of this new sport.

   NOTE: The Random Words can be used in any way: concept, function, association, value, etc.

EXAMPLE

The three Random Words are: OAR; DECOY; PYRAMID.

Thoughts:

. . . "pyramid" suggests a mound which people have to climb to the top of
. . . "oar" suggests a long pole which can be used to prevent others reaching the top. You cannot hit anyone with the pole but you can use it as a barrier
. . . "decoy" suggests a second pyramid. A team can choose to ascend one or other of the mounds
. . . a two-team game of six players in each team. The objective is to reach the top of either mound, where there is a flag to be taken. This counts as one "point" or "goal"
. . . the teams take it in turn to attack and defend. The time to take the flag is noted. If the flag is not taken within a certain time, the other team gets the point

VARIATIONS

1. The design task may be a board game rather than a sport, or any other type of game.
2. You may discard one of the three Random Words and take a further word.

EXERCISE 33

STRONG
CONNECTION

Back to perceptual creativity. This means the creativity of looking at things in multiple ways.

There is also the element of assessing the strength of a connection and distinguishing between a weak (just possible) connection and a strong (dominant) connection.

PROCESS

1. Obtain one Random Word.
2. Obtain further Random Words, one at a time, until you have one which has a strong and obvious connection to the first Random Word.
3. Explain the connection and why you think it is a strong connection.

   NOTE: For each Random Word obtained you can seek to show some connection and explain why you are waiting for a stronger connection.

EXAMPLE

First Random Word: WAGON.

Second Random Word: BUS STATION.

. . . quite a strong connection in terms of transport and travel

Third Random Word: PASSION.

. . . weak connection, possibly "a passion for travel"

Fourth Random Word: OPTIMIST.

. . . weak connection. Anyone who travels is an optimist
   about reaching the destination

Fifth Random Word: GOLF.

. . . good connection in terms of the caddy cart or buggy
   used to move around a golf course

The strongest connection is probably the first one.

VARIATIONS

1. What other possible connections are there between the
   two words that have the strongest connection?
2. Pick five Random Words. Select the two with the
   strongest obvious connection. Seek other connections
   between these chosen two.
3. Obtain two groups of three Random Words each. Find
   the strongest connection between a word in one group
   and a word in the other group.

EXERCISE 34

SNAP

This exercise is derived directly from the Think Link series of the early 1970s.

The emphasis is directly and exclusively on concepts. No other basis for similarity or connection is acceptable.

PROCESS

1. **Obtain one Random Word.**
2. **Obtain further Random Words, one at a time, until a word shows a strong concept similarity with the first word obtained. You may say "snap" if you wish.**
3. **Explain the concept that is similar.**

NOTE: Be very disciplined about the "concept" basis of the exercise.

EXAMPLE

First Random Word: NEON LIGHT.

Second Random Word: CORD.

. . . a cord is long and thin. Neon lights are usually long and
thin (but this is more description than concept)

Third Random Word: ENCYCLOPEDIA.

. . . the purpose of a neon light is usually to impart
information. That is also the purpose of an
encyclopedia

Fourth Random Word: JUICE.

. . . often brightly colored like a neon light (again this is
more descriptive and not part of the function)
. . . would probably stay with "encyclopedia"

VARIATIONS

1. This is ideal as a two-person exercise. Both players are
   waiting to say "snap" when a new Random Word is
   obtained. The person saying "snap" must immediately
   define the concept behind the "snap."
2. Obtain two Random Words each time—even the first
   time. "Snap" can then apply to a concept similarity
   between any one of the original two and any one of
   the two newly obtained words.

BREAK AND BUILD

This exercise contains elements of analysis and constructive thinking. So there is both perceptual creativity and also constructive creativity.

PROCESS

1. Obtain three Random Words.
2. Break each Random Word down into its component parts, whether these are physical parts or abstracted parts. (Concepts, values or functions may be abstracted from the word but are not physical parts of it.)
3. Put as many different parts as you can together to form something that offers value.
4. Explain the value created.

   NOTE: The value created must be realistic. Just being novel is not enough.

EXAMPLE

The three Random Words are: TAXI; GRANNY; TITLE.

Thoughts:

. . . "taxi" might break down into: recognizable vehicle,
transport, driver, fare, taximeter
. . . "granny" might break down into: old age, family, grey
hair, shopping
. . . "title" might break down into: recognizable distinction,
method of address, reward

Idea:

. . . a sort of "granny club" which old people could belong
to. They would have an identification card. All taxi
fares, and other transport fares, would be reduced. This
might also apply to shopping (reasonable amounts)

VARIATIONS

1. Obtain one Random Word. From this, extract some
value. Obtain further Random Words and look to see
how each could help to deliver the selected value.
2. Obtain four Random Words and discard one before
proceeding with the basic exercise.
3. Obtain a further Random Word after designing the idea
and see if this could contribute to the idea.

VALUES

The emphasis is on values. The values might relate to a person, to an organization, to the environment, etc. The values discovered should be as direct as possible.

The ability to see values is a very central part of creativity. Without the ability to see values you would not be able to see the values in any idea you created.

PROCESS

1. **Obtain five Random Words.**
2. **Find the values in each Random Word. There may be more than one value.**
3. **Group the words according to the dominant values. You may include a word in two different groups if the word shows two values.**
4. **Explain the value groupings.**

> **NOTE: There should be a minimum of two words in each grouping.**

EXAMPLE

The five Random Words are: POWER; CAVE; DIAPER; BUTTER; SHOELACE.

Thoughts:

. . . "cave," "diaper" and "shoelace" have a container type of value. They serve to hold things
. . . "power" and "butter" have an energy type of value

VARIATIONS

1. From the obtained Random Words pick out a word which has a unique value that is not shown by any of the others.
2. Continue to obtain Random Words until you have a minimum of three words in each value grouping.

SHOWCASE

How do you demonstrate or showcase a value?

You might be aware of a certain value but how do you demonstrate this to others? This is the role of advertising executives, who have to communicate values.

PROCESS

1. Obtain a single Random Word.
2. Extract the principle value from this Random Word.
3. How would you showcase or demonstrate that value?
4. Obtain a second Random Word. See if the new word can help you in your task of demonstrating the extracted value.

> NOTE: You may demonstrate the value in any way and do not need to remain tied to the Random Word.

EXAMPLE

The Random Word is: SPIT.

Thoughts:

. . . there are two meanings of "spit." One is the stuff that
comes out of your mouth and the other is the rod on
which you barbecue chickens or other items of food
. . . the first value might be "the ability to get rid of stuff
that is not needed and may even be uncomfortable."
This value could be shown using the example of a
person whose life has become cluttered up with things
that are not needed. They need to be discarded. There
are also old laws that need to be discarded. For example,
every taxi cab in London is supposed to carry a bale of
hay (from the days when taxis were horse-drawn)
. . . the second value is "the ability to hold things in a certain
position so that some process can take place." A demon-
stration here could be a plaster cast that holds a leg in
a certain position so that healing of a broken bone can
take place

Further Random Word: EARS.

Thoughts:

. . . to some extent ears are selective and allow us to listen
to some sounds and not others. It would be useful if we
could instruct our ears to block out some sounds
. . . in some animals the ears are very efficiently designed to
allow the source of sounds to be located. This is a type
of positioning to get the best effect

VARIATIONS

1. Suggest an advertising slogan to communicate the chosen value. Possibly even an advertising poster or TV commercial.
2. List existing things that illustrate this particular value.

EXERCISE 38

DESCRIPTION

Indirect descriptions rely on comparisons. In this exercise you are asked to make comparisons between an item and other items in order to define the first item.

There is a creative need to discover the points of comparison that aid the description.

PROCESS

1. Obtain a single Random Word. This is the item that has to be described.
2. Obtain three more Random Words.
3. Describe the first item by reference and comparison to the other three items.

NOTE: Both contrast and similarity may be used.

EXAMPLE

First Random Word: PADDOCK.

Next three Random Words: HIGH JUMP; PADLOCK; PORRIDGE.

Thoughts:

. . . porridge is food contained on a plate. A paddock contains the grass that is food for horses

. . . a padlock locks something at one point. A paddock contains by having a fence around it which locks animals into that area

. . . to win at high jump you have to be able to jump very high. In order for an animal to get out of a paddock the animal would have to jump high over the surrounding fence

VARIATIONS

1. Obtain four Random Words at the same time. Choose the one that is going to be described in terms of the other three.
2. Obtain further Random Words one at a time and see how each could be used to describe the first word in the basic exercise.

POLITICAL POWER

This is another exercise with a very defined task to be achieved. The task is to provide something that would help a political party. This help might be in the form of policy or just as a slogan that could be used.

The purpose of the thinking is to increase the political power of a party.

PROCESS

1. Obtain four Random Words.
2. Extract concepts, values and ideas from any of these Random Words to serve the political purpose.
3. Explain why you believe the suggestions might work.

NOTE: The suggestions should not be too broad, such as: "Politicians try to do the right thing and vitamins are right for you." They need to be more concrete.

EXAMPLE

The four Random Words are: MUSLIM; DESK; FLAGPOLE; QUILT.

Thoughts:

... emphasise the multicultural aspect (Muslim) but at the same time emphasise that all cultures come together in a national identity (flagpole)
... the party is pro-business (desk) but also pro-family and home-owners (quilt)
... note that a quilt can be made up of a variety of different materials which come together to give one quilt. So different cultures can come together to give one nation

VARIATIONS

1. Create an actual election slogan based on the approach derived from the four Random Words.
2. Put together an attacking strategy with which to attack the opposing party—also based on the Random Words.

EXERCISE 40

HISTORY

This exercise involves a rather unusual use of creativity.

History is about truth and the truth of what has happened in the past. But the way we look at the past is also a matter of perception and interpretation. This is where perceptual creativity can come in. Creativity can suggest possibilities which may then be checked out in different ways.

Information may be about facts, but the way the information is seen is a matter of perception.

PROCESS

1. Obtain five Random Words.
2. Examine each of these Random Words to see in what way that word could relate to history. What might the word suggest or contribute?

    NOTE: The ideas may relate to history in general or to particular episodes in history.

EXAMPLE

The five Random Words are: ANGLE; COLOR; IVY;
OLYMPICS; REFEREE.

Thoughts:

... "angle" suggests the particular point of view of a person
  or of an historian
... "color" suggests tinted spectacles and the color or
  prejudice through which history is being examined
... an idea might be to lay out some different possibilities
  of angle and color and to write a history version from
  each of the different angles—instead of presenting one
  version as the truth
... "referee" suggests some body or ombudsman who
  would look at different versions of history and give
  each a seal of approval or condemnation as he or she
  deemed fit. In other words, history is not just the
  possession of historians or the people involved in the
  history. There needs to be an independent objective
  assessment
... "ivy" covers things up and you do not know what is
  underneath. The same cover-up may happen with
  history either deliberately or through circumstances
... the Olympics were a sort of suspension of history when
  the quarrelling states would forget their fights to come
  together to compete in athletics. This added a different
  dimension of competition. Perhaps wars in history
  could be looked at differently—perhaps as the behavior
  of key personalities rather than because of underlying
  causes

VARIATIONS

1. Obtain six Random Words and arrange these in historical order. When did the item, object or concept first appear?
2. Obtain five Random Words as in the basic exercise and then apply them to a particular episode in history, for example: the French Revolution; the formation of the British Empire; the American Civil War, etc.

EXERCISE 41

DIFFERENT
DIRECTIONS

The emphasis is on "difference" and "directions."

Starting from a central point, different roads move out in different directions.

One of the functions of creative thinking is to open up directions different from the usual. These are "possibilities." What we do with those possibilities is another matter.

PROCESS

1. Obtain a single Random Word.
2. Obtain three further Random Words which can be obtained one after the other.
3. Show how each one of the further Random Words can develop, change, improve or otherwise "take forward" the first Random Word.
4. In all cases explain the difference between the three directions of change.

NOTE: Be as specific as possible. Very general statements are not much better than saying you would solve a problem by finding the right answer!

EXAMPLE

First Random Word: BUNDLE.

Next three Random Words: HOLLY; QUEEN; PLAYGROUND.

Thoughts:

... "holly" suggests Christmas and this leads the idea of "bundle" in the direction of a bundle of Christmas needs (or activities). There is a bundle that can be acquired rather than buying things separately
... there might be a bundle of behaviors which are known in advance and which get royal approval and perhaps some royal recognition
... playgrounds designed for a bundle of different activities. There might be a role of playground activator who can introduce and teach different games and activities

VARIATIONS

1. Obtain further Random Words, one at a time, and see whether each one can extend one of the directions already established by the previous Random Words.
2. Obtain four Random Words in the basic exercise and then discard one of them.
3. Try a different starting Random Word and then see how the existing three further words can open up different directions from this new starting point.

EXERCISE 42

OPERATING CONCEPTS

An "operating concept" is very different from a "descriptive concept." An operating concept is concerned with operations and with actions. It is close to a functional concept.

How does this work? How does this operate? How does this produce results?

There is a difference between the details of operation and the concept behind the details. Once the concept has been determined, then that concept can operate through different details.

PROCESS

1. Obtain six Random Words.
2. In how many of these Random Words can you identify a similar operating concept?
3. The similar concept may exist in two or more of the words. There may be different operating concepts that occur in more than one of the words.
4. Spell out the operating concepts very clearly.

NOTE: The search is for a key or basic operating concept. What is the driving concept? Peripheral concepts are not acceptable.

EXAMPLE

The six Random Words are: SPINE; BUS STATION; LOOM; CRASH; QUARRY; BRIDLE.

Thoughts:

. . . "spine" and "bus station" operate as central parts of a communication system
. . . "loom" and "bridle" provide a sort of frame through which human activity can achieve desired results
. . . "quarry" and "crash" both involve the use of considerable force—in one case desired and in the other not desired

VARIATIONS

1. Obtain further Random Words one by one and see if any of them have the same operating concept as those already described.
2. Obtain a single Random Word and define the operating concept. Obtain other Random Words one by one until you find one which shares the same operating concept.

POETRY

This is a direct use of creativity to stimulate an artistic effort: poetry.

In this case, the Random Word provides fixed points in the poem around which the rest can be written.

PROCESS

1. Obtain two Random Words.
2. The first word obtained gives the last word in the first line of a poem.
3. The second line of the poem ends with a word which you choose to rhyme with the first line.
4. The second Random Word forms the last word of the third line in the poem.
5. The fourth line ends with a word you choose to rhyme with the third line.

EXAMPLE

The two Random Words are: SAILOR and PRINCIPAL.

Thoughts:

> She fell in love with a sailor
> No letters did he mail her
> She told the school principal
> Who said the sailor was a "look and see" pal.

VARIATIONS

1. Set up more lines in the poem in the same way.
2. Obtain more Random Words, each of which must occur somewhere in the poem—but not necessarily at the end of a line.

EXERCISE 44

TWINS

This is a matter of matching two words on as many aspects as possible—twinning the words.

The exercise involves perceptual creativity.

PROCESS

1. Obtain five Random Words.
2. From the five words choose two which seem the best matched on several counts.
3. Seek to match on at least three counts.
4. Explain the matching.

   NOTE: As usual, spelling is never accepted as a basis for matching.

EXAMPLE

The five Random Words are: WAGON; SCARF; BINGO; GUITAR; THIEF.

Thoughts:

... "bingo" and "thief" both involve money you have not earned; there is a strong element of uncertainty; happens at night; step-by-step progression; unexpected benefits; morally disapproved of by some

VARIATIONS

1. Draw further words to see if the twins can be turned into triplets.
2. Seek to match two other words in the original five Random Words.

EXERCISE 45

SIMPLIFY

One of the most useful outcomes of applied creativity is simplification. Processes tend to get ever more complex. There is a need to simplify them. Creativity is needed for this simplification.

PROCESS

1. Obtain three Random Words.
2. Obtain another three Random Words.
3. Is there any concept or principle in the second set of three words that can be used to simplify any process in the first set of three words? The item may be used directly or as a concept.
4. Explain the simplification.

NOTE: If the words are totally unsuitable for this process, you may obtain other words. You should, however, make a strong effort to use the words first obtained.

EXAMPLE

First three Random Words: BUS; GRADE; NUMBER.

Second three Random Words: GOSSIP; COLONY; CREDIT CARD.

Thoughts:

. . . the use of credit cards in machines on buses to pay the fare. These could be normal credit cards or special bus credit cards

VARIATIONS

1. Instead of obtaining three Random Words after the first three, obtain one Random Word at a time until you get one which suggests a simplification.
2. Instead of the first three Random Words, obtain Random Words one at a time until you come to a "process" word. You then proceed as above to simplify that process. This is necessary as some words are not suitable for simplification.

EXERCISE 46

SIMILARITY

Creativity opens up options and possibilities. These are essential in any search operation—when we set out to look for something.

In this exercise there is a need to look for something that is similar in some respects.

PROCESS

1. Obtain four Random Words.
2. For each one of these words suggest an animal, bird, fish or insect which is similar in some respect. Humans are excluded.
3. Explain the claimed similarity.
4. If the Random Word is already an animal, etc., then obtain another Random Word.

EXAMPLE

The four Random Words are: PARTNER; JOKE; SNORE;
BIKINI.

Thoughts:

. . . "partner" suggests a long-term relationship. Some birds
(partridges, etc.) mate for life. There is a steady partner
. . . "joke" suggests monkeys who play around as if they had
a sense of fun. Possibly the panda, which looks as if it
were an animal designed as a joke
. . . "snore" suggests the croaking of a frog
. . . "bikini" suggests a wasp or fly with a very tiny waist and
a bulging body above and below—like a well-endowed
woman in a bikini

VARIATIONS

1. Select an animal first and then obtain Random Words
    one by one until you find one which has some
    similarity.
2. Obtain six Random Words and discard two before
    proceeding with the basic exercise.

DEVALUE

What is the key value here? This exercise is all about identifying a key value and then removing that value.

PROCESS

1. Obtain three Random Words.
2. For each of the Random Words, remove one aspect, feature or concept, and by doing so remove the value from the item.
3. Explain why your subtraction devalues the item.

NOTE: Seek to make your subtraction as central as possible. You may only remove one feature or concept.

EXAMPLE

The three Random Words are: NEEDLE; READING; SPACE.

Thoughts:

. . . from "needle" we remove the feature of sharpness. A
blunt needle is not much good
. . . from "reading" we remove knowledge of the language
that is in use. Reading becomes useless. We could also
have removed the legibility of the letters
. . . from "space" we remove the concept of emptiness. If
the space is full of objects we tend not to think of it as
space

VARIATIONS

1. In a sort of reverse exercise, see how many of the
    aspects you can remove without destroying the basic
    function. For example: needles do not have to be made
    of steel.
2. Seek to add something which would increase the value
    of the item.

ADVERTISE

There is a considerable need for creativity in the advertising world. The communication aspect of the creativity is vital. Without it the creativity is useless. There is a need to produce something which is original—but obvious once it has been done.

PROCESS

1. Obtain four Random Words.
2. Select one of the Random Words as the thing that is to be advertised. If none of the words is suitable for this, then obtain another Random Word.
3. See how the remaining words, or one of them, could be used to advertise the selected one.
4. Suggest slogans, posters, TV commercials, etc.

EXAMPLE

The four Random Words are: ICON; TARGET; STAFF; CONSUMER.

Thoughts:

. . . the business to be advertised is an agency providing temporary office staff
. . . the advertisement asks: "Who are the consumers?" of the service. Is it the public? Is it the existing office staff? Is it the employer looking for staff?
. . . the agency lays out its target—what it is trying to do. Maybe this could be providing staff who fit in and are quick to learn
. . . the advertisement seeks to make this agency the icon agency in this business area

VARIATIONS

1. Aim specifically at a slogan, a poster, a headline or a TV commercial.
2. Obtain Random Words one at a time until you have one which is suitable as something to be advertised. Then draw further Random Words, one by one, and show how each could help with the advertising.

ATTRACTIVE

In this exercise, creativity is used to design value. The creative effort is to see how a given something can be used to add value. So there is a need to explore values and possibilities.

PROCESS

1. Obtain five Random Words.
2. See how you could use the concepts, features, associations or physical nature of any one of the five words to increase the attraction of any other one of the five words.
3. Do this for as many of the five words as you can.
4. Explain why you believe there would be an added attractiveness.

   NOTE: Make your values as obvious as possible. They should also apply in most ordinary circumstances and not just in very special circumstances.

EXAMPLE

The five Random Words are: TRAM; NECKLACE; CONGRESS; MELON; PARADE.

Thoughts:

... from "parade" we get the idea that members of Congress should parade down a central street one day a month so the public can see them and comment

... from "melon" we get the idea that if you are walking and eating a melon you need some way of holding the melon—a sort of "necklace" could be used

... from "Congress" we get the idea of a necklace that shows all the political parties—or representatives

... from "tram" we get the idea of parades where people do not march but stand on flat cars on the tramlines and are towed along so people can see them

VARIATIONS

1. Obtain just one Random Word. Then draw further words and see how each one could help to make the first item more attractive.
2. Obtain four Random Words and discard two. The remaining two are used to make more attractive an item shown by a Random Word obtained in advance.
3. Extend the concept of attraction offered by a Random Word to include other ways of carrying out the concept.

GROWTH

Growth means progression in an upward direction. People grow, businesses grow, ideas grow, etc.

The creative task in this exercise is to keep the objective of growth clearly in mind and so see how it might be achieved with the Random Words obtained.

PROCESS

1.   Obtain four Random Words.
2.   Start with the simplest of the words and then proceed step by step to the more complex. Imagine you are growing a business. How would it grow—using the Random Words as stages or steps?
3.   If you find that the first four Random Words are totally unsuitable, then you may obtain four more. But make a strong effort to use the first four—that is the nature of creativity.
4.   Explain the stages of growth and their feasibility.

EXAMPLE

The four Random Words are: SALIVA; SAINT; LICENSE; MENU.

Thoughts:

. . . "saliva" suggests mouths and dentistry
. . . you obtain a license to set up a dental clinic and employ licensed dentists
. . . you grow the business by offering a menu of other types of care, such as plastic surgery
. . . "saint" suggests heaven. So you add a hospice service for those who are terminally ill

VARIATIONS

1. Obtain the Random Words one by one. Use each word as a stage in a business determined by the first word.
2. The first Random Word determines the business. Obtain another Random Word if the first one is totally unsuitable. Then obtain two Random Words together. Choose to use one of them and discard the other. The chosen word should suggest a growth stage in the business.

EXERCISE 51

INFLUENCE

In an interactive world, many things have an influence on other things. The influence may be strong or weak. The influence may be direct or indirect. The influence may be positive or negative.

Exploring the possibilities of influence is another of the tasks of creativity.

PROCESS

1.   Obtain five Random Words.
2.   Show how each of these Random Words might influence the other words in some way.
3.   Explain the influence.

   NOTE: In this exercise, remote types of influence are acceptable.

EXAMPLE

The five Random Words are: HANDBAG; COMET; PEPPER; SNAKE; REFUGEE.

Thoughts:

. . . a snakeskin handbag is highly valued
. . . a pepper spray in the handbag is useful to deter assailants
. . . refugees need large handbags because they may have to carry all their possessions in their bag
. . . refugees crossing a border illegally might be deterred if snakes were placed along the border
. . . refugees might be influenced by a comet or the state of the heavens before setting out on their journey
. . . pepper might, or might not, deter a snake

VARIATIONS

1. Obtain one Random Word. Then obtain three more Random Words. See which of these three would most strongly influence the first word.
2. Obtain two Random Words. Then obtain Random Words one at a time. See how each new word would influence one or both of the first two words—and in what way.
3. Obtain one Random Word. Obtain other Random Words. Decide in advance whether the influence is going to be positive or negative. Then see how the new Random Word can affect the first word in the predetermined manner (positive or negative).

EXERCISE 52

USEFUL

There are many types of beneficial effect. One of them is being useful in a determined situation.

One of the important functions of creativity is to seek out value and to develop "value sensitivity." This is important both for assessing ideas and also for generating them.

PROCESS

1. Obtain four Random Words.
2. Obtain a further Random Word.
3. Seek to show how the last Random Word obtained can be useful with regard to each of the first four words.
4. Explain your suggestions.

   NOTE: "Useful" can be interpreted quite broadly. Any direct beneficial effect would be acceptable. A concept influence would also be acceptable.

EXAMPLE

The four Random Words are: GRANITE; CLAY; SUNGLASSES; MARBLE.

Further Random Word: TROLLEY.

Thoughts:

... a trolley is obviously useful in transporting marble, granite and even clay
... there could be a polishing system attached to a trolley for polishing floors made of granite or marble
... a sort of small hand-held trolley might be of use for rolling or shaping clay in the making of pottery—or to apply a design
... trolleys have four wheels, and this might suggest four lenses for the sunglasses. One possibility might be to have two further lenses which can be fitted over the existing lenses for very bright situations

VARIATIONS

1. Obtain two Random Words. Discard one and use the other.
2. Obtain two Random Words and seek to use both of them.
3. Obtain Random Words one at a time. See how the second word could be useful with the first. Then see how the third word could be useful with the second. Then see how the fourth word could be useful with the third—and so on.

MIDDLE

There is sometimes a need to relate to two different things at the same time. This exercise focuses on that situation.

There is a need to position things so that all the relationships work.

PROCESS

1. Obtain six Random Words.
2. In the final arrangement there are three columns. Each word in the middle column relates to the word at the same level in the first column but also to the word at the same level in the last column.
3. Explain the relationships.

   NOTE: You can wait until you have all six words before constructing the columns.

EXAMPLE

The six Random Words are: BLACKBOARD; PERFUME; LAW; MIDWIFE; LIST; GOAL.

Thoughts:

. . . possible arrangement as shown below:

BLACKBOARD	LIST	LAW
PERFUME	GOAL	MIDWIFE

. . . lists are often put on blackboards; lists are made of cases to be tried in a court

. . . the goal of perfume is to help women; the goal of a midwife is to help women

VARIATIONS

1. Produce the first and last column using the first six Random Words that are obtained. These are fixed and cannot be changed. Obtain further Random Words, one at a time, until there is a word which fits in the middle column. Continue for the next words.
2. Produce the first column, which is fixed. Obtain further Random Words for the second column so that each word relates to the same-level word in the first column. Obtain further Random Words, one at a time, to find words to fit the last column.

TRIANGLE

This is another exercise involving a double relationship. Each word has to relate to two other words.

The format of a triangle is used.

PROCESS

1. Obtain five Random Words.
2. From these select three words which are to form the triangle. The other two can be discarded.
3. Each word is at a corner of the triangle and must relate to the other words at the other points on the triangle.
4. Explain the relationships.

> NOTE: The process is quite hard with a limited number of words, so the relationship might be quite remote. But try for a strong one.

EXAMPLE

The five Random Words are: RING; CLOUD; HUNT; GIRDERS; SALE.

Thoughts:

. . . "hunt" is at the top of the triangle. "Ring" and "sale" are at the base points
. . . the wedding ring signifies the end of the hunt (for both parties)
. . . during the hunt, both groom and bride are on sale
. . . the groom might seek to find a ring in a sale and so save some money

VARIATIONS

1. Obtain five more words. You may use the side of an existing triangle to make a new triangle with a new word (which must relate to each word with which it is connected by a line). "A–B–C" might be an existing triangle and "B–C–E" a new triangle.
2. Obtain six Random Words and arrange them as pairs. Obtain further Random Words, one at a time, and seek to change the pairs into triangles.

EXERCISE 55

OBVIOUS

There are obvious relationships and other relationships which are not so obvious. We need to be aware of the obvious relationships even when we seek to go beyond the obvious. It would never make sense to deliberately ignore the obvious.

PROCESS

1. Obtain five Random Words.
2. Which one of these five words relates in the most obvious fashion to one other of the five words?
3. Which of the five words does not seem to relate to any other of the five words?
4. Explain the relationships.

EXAMPLE

The five Random Words are: NEST; NURSE; BATTERY;
STOCK MARKET; TAPE.

Thoughts:

. . . "tape" relates to "stock market" (ticker tape). "Tape"
relates to "battery," as in the need for batteries in a
tape recorder. Nurses use tape for a variety of
reasons—including surgical tape. Birds would probably
use tape to hold a nest together—if they could
. . . the least relating word might be "battery," which only
relates directly to "tape"

VARIATIONS

1. Seek some form of relationship between each of the
   five Random Words. Classify each relationship as
   strong, weak or remote.
2. Obtain further Random Words, one at a time, until you
   find one which relates obviously to all five words.

EXERCISE 56

RESCUE

This is a form of problem-solving involving rescue. There is a difficult situation and you have to find a way out of it—using one of the Random Words you obtain.

There is a need both for flexible thinking and also for focused thinking.

PROCESS

1. **Obtain five Random Words.**
2. **Use one of the Random Words to suggest a problem or crisis.**
3. **Use a different Random Word to suggest how the situation can be rescued and things put right.**
4. **Explain your thinking.**

EXAMPLE

The five Random Words are: HEAT; BROOCH; PASSION; WORM; TUSK.

Thoughts:

. . . there is a crisis of passion. A young lady is not very pleased with her young man, who has gone out with another woman
. . . the situation is rescued by the gift of a diamond brooch from the young man to his lady

VARIATIONS

1. Obtain a further Random Word and use this to generate a new difficulty which must be rescued using the first five words.
2. Use two of the Random Words to solve the problem.

EXERCISE 57

MULTIPLY

This exercise involves free-flowing associations and concepts. The emphasis is on expansion and possibilities—even if remote.

PROCESS

1. Obtain three Random Words.
2. For each of these Random Words produce 10 more words which are related in some way to that word. This may be by association, concept, value, components, etc.

NOTE: The closer the relationship the better. To say that two items are related because both can be found in shops is rather weak.

EXAMPLE

The three Random Words are: THREAT; PIN-UP; BELLOWS.

Thoughts:

. . . for "bellows" we might have: fire; air; energize; oxygen; pump; combustion; steel-making; human energy; timing; control
. . . for "pin-up" we might have: glamor; magazine; girl; attraction; sex; beauty; aspiration; image; role model; pose
. . . for "threat" we might have: pressure; force; demand; blackmail; future problem; believable or not; hidden or obvious; known person or not; credibility; time scale

VARIATIONS

1. Allow each Random Word to generate only three new words. But each of the new words must generate three more words. And one more time.
2. Permit only "action words."

EXERCISE 58

KEEP GOING

Another exercise that focuses on strong connections. But you have to find the connections. They may not all be obvious. There may be value connections, concepts connections, use connections, etc.

PROCESS

1. Obtain a single Random Word.
2. Obtain a second Random Word. If you can show a strong connection to the first Random Word, keep going and draw another Random Word.
3. So long as you can show a strong connection to the preceding word, you continue.
4. Explain your connections.

   NOTE: It is up to you to decide that your connection is not very strong and so end the exercise.

EXAMPLE

First Random Word: WAITER.

Second Random Word: WASP.

Connection:

. . . they both hang around food and are both well dressed

Third Random Word: GRANNY.

Connection:

. . . to "wasp": can be sharp and acute mentally and able to inflict damage

Fourth Random Word: TOWER.

Connection:

. . . possibly that a granny can be a tower of strength. This is weak, so the exercise ends

VARIATIONS

1. Obtain two Random Words at a time but only use one of them and discard the other.
2. Run two separate exercises, or lines, in parallel. Add the new word to one or the other.

EXERCISE 59

AUTOMATE

What can be automated?

You need to think of value and feasibility.

You need to think how something would work out in practice.
Is it worth doing?

PROCESS

1. Obtain four Random Words.
2. For each of the Random Words see if the whole process
    or some key function could be automated.
3. What would the value be?

EXAMPLE

The four Random Words are: PLASTIC; CRASH; CLOWN; TAXI.

Thoughts:

. . . the process of manufacturing plastics is already largely
automated
. . . some automatic sensing device in a car which can
predict imminent crashes and take preventive action.
This might not apply to all crashes but could, for
example, prevent crashes resulting from the driver
falling asleep
. . . robot clowns in shopping centers. Such clowns could tell
jokes and reply to simple questions with a funny
answer—from a standard repertoire
. . . automated ordering and routing of taxis. A direct credit-
card-accepting system in the taxi itself

VARIATIONS

1. Look to see if there is a function common to all four
   Random Words that can be automated.
2. Obtain six Random Words and discard two of them.
3. Could a cell phone help with any of the functions of the
   Random Words obtained?

EXERCISE 60

FAIRY STORY

You are writing a fairy tale for children. How would you incorporate features produced randomly? How might they help the story?

PROCESS

1. Obtain four Random Words.
2. Incorporate these four words in a children's story.

> NOTE: The story must include all four items as such—not just a concept derived from the Random Word. It is not enough to say that Peter walked down the road and saw A and then saw B, etc. The items must be fully incorporated.

EXAMPLE

The four Random Words are: BOUTIQUE; COUGH MEDICINE; VERSE; SAUNA.

Thoughts:

. . . Lucy had a bad cough and needed to take cough medicine. It tasted awful. Her mother told her that if she did not take the medicine she might have to sit in a sauna to help her cough. Lucy hated this even more— all that hot steam and stuff. She had an idea. She suggested that for every spoonful of medicine she should get some points. When she had enough points they would go to the boutique and buy some fancy clothes. If her mother did not like the idea she would have to say why she did not like the idea in verse. Lucy got her way. But she did take the medicine

VARIATIONS

1. Once you have the story, obtain a further Random Word and seek to fit it into the story.
2. Obtain six Random Words, then discard two and use the remaining four.

EXERCISE 61

PART

Things exist in their own right but they could also form part of something else. Part of the process of design is to put things together to deliver value.

In this exercise you need to see if something could be part of something else—and if it would add value.

PROCESS

1. Obtain five Random Words.
2. See whether any one of these words (the item) could form an actual part of the operation of any other of the words.
3. Explain your thinking and show value.

NOTE: As far as possible the item should be used directly and not just a concept from the item. The use should show some increased value.

EXAMPLE

The five Random Words are: LASER; TOAST; EYEBROW;
KISS; TOES.

Thoughts:

. . . a laser might form part of a toaster to tell whether the
toast was ready or not
. . . eyebrows or toes might form part of a kiss if the kiss
was directed that way
. . . laser trimming of toenails might be a remote possibility

VARIATIONS

1. If the original Random Words do not seem suitable,
    obtain five new ones.
2. Obtain one Random Word. Continue to obtain others,
    one at a time, until you find a word which could
    become part of the first one obtained.

EXERCISE 62

HEADLINES

Another design exercise. Headlines have to be informative, they have to catch attention, and they should be intriguing. The various articles may be the same but the headlines can make all the difference.

PROCESS

1. **Obtain four Random Words.**
2. **Write a newspaper headline which directly incorporates two of the Random Words. You may choose the situation.**

   NOTE: The words have to be used directly in their original form.

EXAMPLE

The four Random Words are: DANCE; WORD; BAR; ADDRESS.

Thoughts:

... THE DANCE AT THE WRONG ADDRESS. A bunch of
people turned up at the wrong address for a dance.
There was a dance there but not the one they thought.
There was a scuffle which turned into a major fight and
the police had to be called
... THE BAR WITHOUT A WORD. A bartender decided to
introduce a "silent hour." During that hour customers
could drink as much as they liked but could not talk.
They could use sign language if they wished. The
consumption of beer increased dramatically
... THE USUAL DANCE OF WORDS. The communiqué
released at the end of a negotiating conference was full
of words but said little. It was described by the minister
for external affairs as "the usual dance of words"

VARIATIONS

1. Try to incorporate three or even four of the words in
    your headline.
2. Choose one of the obtained words to include in your
    headline. Then obtain two more Random Words which
    also have to be included.
3. Use one of the Random Words to suggest the situation
    about which the headline is being written.

TABLES OF RANDOM WORDS

Table 1

	1	2	3
1	BRAKES	SHARK	SNAIL
	PARACHUTE	WELL	SOAP
	ROAD SIGN	BOMB	BATH
	SMILE	TONGUE	TROPHY
	CLOUD	EARS	RACE
	TOOTH	RADIO	ENERGY
2	VOTE	KNIFE	TOES
	PAIL	SOUP	MASSAGE
	JUMP	ICE CREAM	PEN
	NEWSPAPER	TELEPHONE	FLAG
	FROG	SHOUT	SARDINE
	SEA	LAWYER	SAUCE
3	ICE	BRIDGE	LETTER
	HORSE	DIVER	COMPUTER
	EXAM	CANE	FUNERAL
	ROBOT	SUGAR	PARADE
	TV	MOUSE	BAND
	CUP	FLEA	DRUM
4	GRASS	KING	BARRIER
	SNAKE	CARPET	PICNIC
	BALLROOM	TRUMPET	BEER
	KEY	LAMP	BEGGAR
	PENCIL	WIRE	CRUTCH
	COURT	HAMMER	BEARD
5	BOOK	DOOR	HEADLINE
	PRISON	ROOF	SACK
	DANCE	STAIRS	POTATO
	FOOD	GARDEN	DAISY
	SHOP	CHAIR	CIGARETTE
	TOWER	CIRCUS	LIPSTICK
6	SHEET	CLOWN	NOSE
	PICTURE	POLITICIAN	SHOES
	ROSE	DESK	STRING
	CACTUS	BRIBE	PRISON
	DESERT	POLICEMAN	BATH
	FISH	STATUE	SALT

4	5	6
ISLAND	CELL PHONE	MANNERS
TOOTHPICK	ADVERTISING	THREAT
BACTERIA	BAR	INSULT
HEADACHE	STEERING WHEEL	SUBMARINE
PLANE	WHEELCHAIR	OSTRICH
WINDOW	HOSPITAL	GIRAFFE
TENNIS	PILL	UNIVERSITY
BALL	MIDWIFE	PHARMACY
FUR	MAGAZINE	NECK
SMOKE	PIN-UP	KISS
GLASSES	MOUSE	ELEPHANT
WHISKY	CAFÉ	THEATER
JAZZ	RACE	SOLDIER
OPERA	LADDER	SKYSCRAPER
CHANDELIER	WAR	TRAIN
GHOST	CURRY	ELEVATOR
CHURCH	FUNGUS	WINE
SAINT	LIPSTICK	STOMACH
CARPENTER	ZOO	RASH
SAW	CORNER	TRAPEZE
SCREWDRIVER	DICE	LAW
SAND	GAMBLE	JOKE
VOLCANO	CHRISTMAS	MOSQUITO
BEACH	VACATION	FIREWORKS
BIKINI	CHEWING GUM	SHADOW
BABY	BELL	PAIN
MOON	TABLE	LAUGH
WINE	COFFEE	TOMB
BREAD	CARNIVAL	FOAM
HAIR	CRUISE SHIP	WAVE
CHEESE	CHOCOLATE	BOXING
CAT	WEDDING	CROWN
DINOSAUR	SNORE	SCHOOL
KANGAROO	BIRD	DICTIONARY
FIRE	GOLF	BANK
WIND	FORK	FAN

Table 2

	1	2	3
1	WALLET SAUSAGE EAGLE STRING EGG OYSTER	CHICKEN TYPEWRITER BLANKET SWIMMING POOL TEA POT PEPPER	TOURIST SAILOR SCREW SLIPPER YACHT NEEDLE
2	PILOT BRICK FIREMAN ENGINEER CRANE HOOK	BUTTER DENTIST MARBLE MASK SWING STOCK MARKET	INTERNET SIEVE TRAFFIC LIGHTS STARS CHAIN ARROW
3	SNAIL SAUCEPAN NECKLACE BEAD SPOON DISH	RAILWAY SONG SEESAW THERMOMETER SCISSORS TILE	PROFIT HOPE TAX SOCCER SMOKE TAR
4	PUPPET CALCULATOR CARD HAND OVEN REFEREE	JACKET BELT BUTTON ZIP NAPKIN BOTTLE	DRAGON SAFE INK STADIUM CAROUSEL PIANO
5	ATHLETICS BEER PUB RADIATOR PICTURE ENVELOPE	RIVER SALMON LABEL CD MICROPHONE SPINE	MEDAL FRIES FROST BANANA ELECTION EPIDEMIC
6	LOAN SHARK FLEA MARKET HAMBURGER POSTER	CUSTARD CRYSTAL LOOM WHISTLE NUTS ASPIRIN	DONKEY CARRIAGE SWORD KITE TIE GYM

4	5	6
CHOIR	TRUCK	PRANK
TIRE	SKATEBOARD	KETCHUP
SPIRE	TURKEY	CONCERT
MUD	PANCAKE	LINE
CLIFF	RADAR	SHEET
MOLE	PLASTIC	BULB
CHIMNEY	SWITCH	TORTOISE
KITCHEN	SURVEY	LASER
BOARD	BELLY BUTTON	CURTAIN
BEE	ANGEL	TICKET
JOURNALIST	SENTRY	BUS
SCORPION	BISHOP	BULLET
TUNNEL	MAGICIAN	RIOT
WIG	LOLLIPOP	FAMILY
SANDALS	VASE	CORPORATION
MOUSTACHE	COMB	GANG
FROWN	RAZOR	DIVING BOARD
PILLOW	TELESCOPE	GNOME
OCTOPUS	PLANET	HINGE
BAR	SPAGHETTI	PANTS
JUDGE	BACON	WARSHIP
REPORT	MUSHROOM	PIGEON
PARROT	SEED	GENERAL
COFFIN	CAMEL	SPY
BIRTHDAY	TANK	PEBBLE
APPLAUSE	KNITTING	NETWORK
DIARY	PERFUME	BULLY
SHELF	MOSS	THUNDER
MICROSCOPE	GUITAR	STORM
FAIRY	ROULETTE	HAYSTACK
GIANT	WHEELBARROW	SADDLE
BULLFIGHT	SCARECROW	TAIL
SATELLITE	HONEY	SPIDER
RUMOR	CEREAL	PYRAMID
TISSUE	MUSTARD	LIBRARY
COAL	DOCK	TOY

Table 3

	1	2	3
1	PUMPKIN ROLLERCOASTER NANNY COW MILKSHAKE STRATEGY	SAXOPHONE ZEBRA BADGE LICENCE SUICIDE WHALE	MUSLIM TRACTOR LADYBIRD CHERRY NUN OATH
2	PENSION POSTBOX PRAIRIE PASTA PUDDING PASSION	BOOTS UNIFORM CAPTAIN TARGET GOWN ORANGE	STAPLE CEILING FIREPLACE CUPBOARD UMBRELLA TENT
3	TAPESTRY SOFA EXECUTIVE FAX COURIER CONFERENCE	SALE PAPER BAG X-RAY TRAP NURSE MEDICINE	CANDLE FILE VIDEO CHESS BUTTON NEWS
4	STATION SPACE POCKET POWDER STAR COMET	COPIER FILM SPEAKER LEADER COOK ALARM	SAUCER PUBLICITY CURTAIN SPOTLIGHT SHOEHORN CONGRESS
5	GEARS SPRING WATERFALL FOREST TIGER MONKEY	MUSTARD LOBSTER HANDKERCHIEF SNEEZE FEVER COUGH	TRAY SUNSET RING COMMITTEE OFFER ALUMINIUM
6	MATCH GOAL DRAW CROWD TOFFEE GARBAGE	BOX LAUNDRY GRADE STAIN OIL CAN	BUNDLE SOFTWARE COMEDY TRAGEDY FROTH IRON

4	5	6
JAY	POTTERY	BRASS
DOUGHNUT	SHRIMPS	LEATHER
BAY	RUDDER	CELLAR
SEAWEED	SAIL	TOOTHBRUSH
MERMAID	OAR	STOOL
CRAB	MAST	PRINTER
COCKROACH	DRUG	COCKTAIL
INK	WAITER	WAGON
SKIN	JET	KIDNAP
SCALES	HOSEPIPE	CELLAR
BARGAIN	BARREL	COACH
ATTIC	TAP	SKYLIGHT
CONSUMER	GUARANTEE	MINT
CLOSET	STAMP	COIN
CASHIER	ADDRESS	POCKET
STORE	BICYCLE	SHOELACE
FOUNDATION	PRIZE	SPIKE
FORMULA	BONUS	MAT
ITALY	VIOLIN	VALLEY
INDIA	GUILLOTINE	CABBAGE
EGYPT	SLIDE	CUCUMBER
CHINA	BROOCH	MELON
FRANCE	PAPERCLIP	THISTLE
RUSSIA	NAIL	TORNADO
WOOL	CAP	PHOTOGRAPH
DANGER	ORDER	VELCRO
HOPE	PACKAGE	CARROT
CREDIT CARD	PROMOTION	SHOWCASE
CHEQUE	GLOVES	REJECT
FASHION	EYEBROW	SCREEN
CONCIERGE	PADLOCK	PARKING METER
HANGER	PEPPER	BUOY
LUGGAGE	BALCONY	SALAD
TRADE	MATTRESS	PRESS
FERRY	SCREAM	SOCKS
BRA	SIGN	BELT

Table 4

	1	2	3
1	APPLE PIE ROSES GUTTER PSYCHIATRIST BUTCHER PORRIDGE	EXAM TEST MUSCLE STAMINA BAIT SPARROW	KENNEL WAREHOUSE CEMETERY GONDOLA BATON CONDUCTOR
2	COTTAGE HORSESHOE MOTH GENERATOR FUSE MOTORCYCLE	PLUG BASIN CLIPPERS FRAME TOAST BLACKBOARD	ORCHESTRA HYMN SERMON POEM BEANS SPINACH
3	AMBULANCE AERIAL COMPASS GALLERY PALACE FRIDGE	HIGH JUMP NEON LIGHT CODE ALPHABET THERMOSTAT CURLERS	CAPITAL POVERTY AID RESCUE RIDDLE RHYTHM
4	PAJAMAS SEAL BASKET LEMONADE UNION BENCH	TRAM MANURE BUS STATION RUNWAY METAL DETECTOR NAIL VARNISH	NEST NIGHT DIAPER NORTH NET NILE
5	ASYLUM KITTEN THRONE BULLDOZER MINER FLORIST	ENCYCLOPEDIA MENU RAVIOLI FLYWHEEL AMPLIFIER ALBUM	MACHINE MONSTER MULBERRY MITE MALE MESS
6	ROCKING CHAIR BRIEFCASE SHIRT SKIRT PLIERS CHAMELEON	SINGER CRIPPLE RANK PRIZE CORD STICKY TAPE	STONE SYSTEM SILO SANITY SHAPE SHORTS

4	5	6
POISON	VOTING	TROLLEY
TONIC	CLIMBING	SHOPPING CENTER
SEDATIVE	SUMMIT	SHOPPING
CAFFEINE	BACKPACK	RESTING
CHAMPAGNE	NIB	MOTEL
VITAMINS	TRAILER	SERVICE
TITLE	BOXING GLOVES	INDIAN
DANCE	MIRROR	COWBOY
GENIUS	REMOTE CONTROL	LASSO
CHEAT	EATING	TEXAS
COPYRIGHT	SWIMMING	CAVE
COMPOSER	SHOOTING	ALGAE
CLASS	OLD MAN	FIGHT
CERTIFICATE	PROPHET	PEACE
PEANUT	THIEF	INSULT
CHIPS	WINNER	REVENGE
COAT	PRIDE	FLIGHT
CLUB	FALL	ATTACK
NEWS	SPACECRAFT	GIRDERS
PLANNING	BALANCE SHEET	DIGGING
TRAINING	RUMOR	SCAFFOLD
MAP	GOSSIP	MAT
WEATHER	FACT	CONCRETE
RAIN	PREJUDICE	ARCHITECT
SNOW	NOISE	GARDEN
FOG	SILENCE	FOUNTAIN
BLISTER	CALM	GATE
SUNBURN	JUSTICE	TRELLIS
LASER	DIVORCE	VINE
SUNGLASSES	JEALOUSY	FERTILIZER
ACCOUNTANT	WORM	COUGH MEDICINE
FLAMENCO	TURF	LAXATIVE
FOREST	FLOWERPOT	SCARF
MEADOW	HOLLY	SOCKS
STREAM	IVY	WALKING STICK
PEBBLE	HAWK	TOILET PAPER

Table 5

	1	2	3
1	SOW	ANKLE	BINDER
	SOUVENIR	ANGLE	BINGE
	SPADE	BOWL	BRIDLE
	RIB	BOW	CHIP
	SPARK	BOUTIQUE	CHIMPANZEE
	WRENCH	CROISSANT	CHIME
2	SQUARE	ESTATE	CULT
	STAFF	ESSAY	CUBE
	STAGE	ESCAPE	CUFF
	REASON	HERB	DUCK
	RECEIPT	HERALD	DEGREE
	READING	HERETIC	EARTH
3	LAP	LADDER	DYNAMO
	JUICE	LIGHTER	ELASTIC
	JUNK	LIGHTHOUSE	EGO
	JUDO	NAVEL	EMERALD
	FACTORY	NUMBER	FAINT
	FAIR	NURSERY	FAIRY TALE
4	EVENING	FAITH	HAIL
	EVIL	FINGER	VACATION
	DOCTRINE	SLED	HAM
	DECOY	FLASHBULB	LOAF
	CAPE	GOOSE	LOFT
	CLOVE	GRANITE	LODGER
5	CHINA	GRADUATE	MISER
	CLOAK	HUNT	MISTAKE
	CLAY	IDIOT	MODEL
	CHINTZ	ICON	PADDOCK
	CHART	INN	PAD
	GREASE	INJURY	PEACOCK
6	BINGO	INVENTION	QUAIL
	AROMA	JOY	QUARRY
	ARSENIC	KID	QUEEN
	ANT	LIMIT	QUILT
	ALTAR	LOUT	RECIPE
	GRAPH	LUNATIC	RESULT

4	5	6
NOUN	FLEET	CRISIS
NOVEL	FINANCE	DECORATOR
NOVICE	FLESH	ARTILLERY
PORCH	FRIAR	ARTIST
PARK	FROCK	BIB
PARTY	GRANNY	BIBLE
PERCH	BREATH	CANCER
PILE	BEAST	CAPER
PIE	BREEZE	COLLEGE
PILLAR	BUSH	COLONY
PIN	BUTTER	CORONATION
PIMPLE	CANNON	CORONET
CONTRACT	LEAF	HEADLINE
CORN	LEMON	HAZARD
CORPSE	LOCUST	MICROBE
COT	LORD	MADMAN
COURTESAN	LOOP	MORNING
COURAGE	LUNCH	MORALS
COMIC	SPAR	PLATE
COMMANDER	STILETTO	PLANET
COLOR	BABOON	SALON
CRUMBS	BLAME	SALIVA
CRY	CABIN	SALARY
CRUST	TARTAN	SALE
ENTRANCE	BUBBLE	TAPE
ENZYME	INTERLUDE	STAMPEDE
ERROR	MUSIC	STARDOM
ESCALATOR	COMET	TOURIST
EXILE	BLONDE	TOWER
FAD	BIBLE	TORTURE
FATIGUE	CHISEL	TOUR
FAULT	LOVER	TURTLE
FARE	OLIVE	TUSK
FARM	POWER	TASK
FATHER	CRITIC	WOOD
FEAST	VALUE	WORD

Table 6

	1	2	3
1	DUTY	SKY	PRINCIPAL
	DUSK	SIGNATURE	PRINTER
	DENIM	RAINCOAT	PROFIT
	FIGURE	PRIEST	SAVIOR
	FILE	PRICE	SAUSAGE
	FIN	PARANOIA	SENATOR
2	GAME	MANHOLE	SURGEON
	GALAXY	IMMIGRANT	SUPPLIES
	GALLOWS	GINGER	SURFACE
	GARLIC	GAS	TRAP
	JUG	FORCE	TERMITE
	JURY	FLIRT	TRAVEL
3	KIDNEY	EMPIRE	HOSTAGE
	LIDO	DODGEM	RANSOM
	LUMP	CROWN	HORSEPOWER
	MESSAGE	CIDER	HOSPITAL
	MEMORY	CHAPEL	HOUR
	MERIT	BLOOD	HORN
4	WALTZ	BANDIT	LEAF
	T-SHIRT	REHEARSAL	LAY-BY
	SUMMER	PLAYGROUND	LAWN
	SUGAR	BUTTERFLY	LEAD
	REBEL	CATERPILLAR	LEECH
	PIRATE	CORK	LENTIL
5	PASSPORT	BENEFIT	LEISURE
	MYTH	BELLOWS	SOLE
	MUTTON	DOVE	LENS
	MIME	DOLPHIN	LEGEND
	MILE	DRINKING	HOBBY
	LODGE	GUIDE	LANE
6	KIPPER	GUILT	LOG
	KIOSK	GUITAR	MILL
	JOINT	MEASURE	MIDGET
	JOKE	OLYMPICS	MIGRAINE
	HYGIENE	PEAR	MIND
	HANDBAG	PEA	MINUTE

4	5	6
PARADISE	ANTIQUE	HARP
PANTHER	ARITHMETIC	GRASSHOPPER
PASTRY	SKI	PRESIDENT
PANTS	APPETITE	MESSENGER
PARASITE	APPLAUSE	HOT PLATE
PARISH	ARCH	STRAW
PARLOR	AQUARIUM	CURL
PARENT	ARM	BUS STOP
REFUGEE	ARMS	BANDAGE
REFERENDUM	ARTHRITIS	PLASTER
REFORM	ASHES	STEW
REINDEER	ASS	ONION
REGION	BERRY	CRASH
REMEDY	ICEBERG	STRETCHER
COUSIN	BEETLE	HELP
RELIGION	BET	ACCIDENT
REPUBLIC	BILL	SHAMPOO
RESEARCH	BIN	VARNISH
SEX	VALUE	POKER
SEASICK	VAN	SLOT MACHINE
SEAGULL	VEGETABLE	BARBER
SEAT	VERSE	VINEGAR
SEARCH	VET	PINCER
SECOND	VICE	GRAFFITI
SECTION	WIDOW	PURSE
SPONGE	WISDOM	CREAM
SPIT	WITCH	TIDE
SPIRIT	WOLF	FLOOD
TATTOO	WORRY	TSUNAMI
TART	WORK	SQUID
TEAR	SATAN	ANCHOR
TAX	SCAR	FALSE TEETH
TAXI	SCALLOP	RHINOCEROS
TEACHER	SCANDAL	REWARD
TEA BAG	SCARF	PUNISHMENT
TEDDY BEAR	SCHEDULE	END

NUMBER
MAPS

6	5	4	3	2	1
3	5	6	1	4	2
2	4	6	1	5	6
1	3	4	2	5	6
2	4	5	3	1	6
4	2	1	5	6	3
5	2	6	3	1	4
3	2	1	5	6	4
6	5	3	1	2	4
6	3	2	1	4	5
2	5	3	6	2	1
4	1	2	5	3	6
5	4	3	2	6	1
6	1	4	2	3	5
4	1	6	3	2	5
2	5	4	3	1	6

1	2	3	4	5	6
6	2	3	1	5	4
5	4	3	2	1	6
1	3	5	2	6	4
6	4	5	2	1	3
3	2	4	6	5	1
6	5	4	3	1	2
2	4	3	5	1	6
3	1	2	6	5	4
5	4	2	3	6	1
4	6	5	2	1	3
2	1	3	5	4	6
2	3	4	5	6	1
6	3	1	2	5	4
1	6	5	3	4	2

TABLES OF
RANDOM
NUMBERS

Reading across the tables, there are four numbers in each row. These are the four numbers you need to access the random word tables.

(If you have used up these tables and wish to reuse them, do so by changing one number in each sequence.)

1	3	6	1			5	1	1	3
3	5	5	5			2	2	3	4
3	1	4	6			5	5	1	5
1	5	6	4			1	2	2	1
5	5	5	5			1	2	3	3

5	4	6	3			5	5	5	1
5	2	1	2			4	4	3	6
2	4	3	5			4	3	2	6
6	5	4	3			4	6	3	5
6	2	6	5			1	2	2	5

5	1	4	5			6	2	4	1
2	5	4	5			1	5	4	2
2	1	1	1			6	2	4	3
6	1	4	5			4	3	2	3
6	5	6	4			1	1	1	5

2 6 5 3	5 4 6 3	1 4 5 3
1 4 3 4	5 5 3 2	4 1 6 2
4 2 4 1	2 3 3 6	5 3 5 1
4 1 6 1	2 4 6 2	4 6 1 2
2 6 5 4	3 3 6 3	2 1 1 1

6 1 4 1	4 3 3 3	3 4 1 6
1 5 2 5	2 5 2 5	6 6 3 2
1 6 6 4	5 5 6 6	1 2 1 1
5 5 3 6	6 4 3 3	1 3 1 6
2 5 1 5	5 1 2 4	4 5 2 2

2 4 2 4	6 4 2 4	5 6 1 2
5 6 6 3	5 1 5 4	3 2 6 1
6 6 4 3	4 4 4 5	3 2 4 5
5 5 5 4	6 3 2 3	2 6 5 3
3 5 4 2	4 6 6 2	5 1 3 1

PRE-SET
TABLE

By inserting any number from 1 to 6 in the space you get a different set of the four numbers needed to access the random word tables.

```
1   6 3        2 4   6            3 2 1
6 4   3          5 3 5          2 3 5
5   2 6        2 1   2          2   4 4
  5 4 4        4   4 6          1 3 6
4 6   4          2 3 1          6 5   3


1 5 4            3 2 1          2   4 4
5 6   3        2   3 2          1 4   1
  6 4 3        5   5 3          6 4   3
5 5   1          2 6 6          1   5 5
  5 2 4        3 1   2            1 4 1


  2 1 5        2   6 3          4 2   6
1 3 6            4 2 2          6   6 1
5 5   1        4   3 4            6 3 1
1 4   5          1 2 2          4 5 3
6   6 5        1 3   5            2 3 1


  3 2 2        1   5 1          5 6   1
2   4 3        5 1 1            5 2   3
  6 5 3        2   6 6            5 1 3
5 3   4          5 6 5          4 2   5
3   3 6        3 3 2              1 5 6
```

ABOUT THE AUTHOR

Edward de Bono is the leading authority in the field of creative thinking and the direct teaching of thinking as a skill. While there are thousands of people writing software for computers, Edward de Bono is the pioneer in writing software for the human brain. From an understanding of how the human brain works as a self-organizing information system, he derived the formal creative tools of lateral thinking. He is also the originator of "parallel thinking" and the Six Thinking Hats. His tools for perceptual thinking (CoRT and DATT) are widely used in both schools and business.

Edward de Bono's instruction in thinking has been sought by many of the leading corporations in the world, such as IBM, Microsoft, Prudential, BT (U.K.), NTT (Japan), Nokia (Finland) and Siemens (Germany). The Australian national cricket team also sought his help and became the most successful cricket team in history.

A group of academics in South Africa included Dr. de Bono as one of the 250 people who had most influenced humanity in the whole course of history. A leading Austrian business journal chose him as one of the 20 visionaries alive today. The leading consultancy company, Accenture, chose him as one of the 50 most influential business thinkers today.